The Complete Ropes Course Manual

Second Edition

Written, Compiled, and Edited by

Karl Rohnke

Catherine M. Tait

Jim B. Wall

Cornerstone Design, Inc.

KENDALL/HUNT PUBLISHING COMPANY
4050 Westmark Drive   Dubuque, Iowa 52002

Cover design by John Scott. Cover photo image © PhotoDisc, Inc.
Chapter one, two and three photographs by Jay Moore.
Chapter three illustrations by Melody Eady.
Chapter four photographs by David Klim.
Chapter two, five, and eight illustrations by Plynn Williams.
Pages iv, v, vi, x, xii, xiv, 2, 5, 8, 20, 62, 65, and 86 photographs by Karl Rohnke.

Previously titled *Ropes Course Manual*
by Jim B. Wall and Catherine M. Tait.

Copyright © 1994, 1997 by Cornerstone Design, Inc.

ISBN 0-7872-2831-1

Printed in the United States of America.

10 9 8 7 6

Cornerstone Design, Inc.

P.O. Box 2082, Milledgeville, Georgia 31061
1-912-454-8333

Feasibility Study

A feasibility study is the first step in obtaining a Ropes Course. It begins with needs assessment interviews with key personnel to clearly elicit the goals, objectives, requirements and limitations of populations being served and to ascertain the most effective way to accomplish this, given site and budget parameters. Next, this data is formulated into a report which is utilized for procurement and justification purposes. This study details all aspects of Ropes Course operation.

Site Survey and Course Design

The site survey and course design reflect usage requirements determined in the feasibility study. The site survey and design service include: site inspection, determination of the course layout, flagging of trees, creation of a course map and a videotape of the site.

Measurements are taken and compiled into complete parts lists. Material specifications sheets reflect latest industry standards in safety, materials, and construction practices. This information is provided in a format that can be directly sent to construction contractors for bidding.

Course Construction

Our experienced, professional staff design and build low and high, multi-element Ropes Courses.

Our construction techniques reflect the latest industry standards and we utilize the highest quality materials available.

We are known for our quick turnaround time and our accessibility before, during, and after completion of your Ropes Course construction project.

Staff Safety Training

Cornerstone Design, Inc. offers an evolving, year round training schedule for staff development. Many programs can be facilitated at your site.

We customize training to meet the requirements of your organization. Workshop topics include: comprehensive safety and rescue techniques, risk management, leadership development, and facilitation skill development.

Advanced Facilitation

Advanced facilitation skills are essential to achieving maximum outcomes on the Ropes Course, as well as in any other adventure program. In recent years, the communications field has begun to merge with the outdoor adventure industry.

We specialize in offering you the best processing skill development available.

Learn simple and effective techniques that will increase your ability to be an elegant catalyst for change and growth.

Safety Inspections

For any Ropes Course to be well maintained, it is beneficial to have fresh and qualified eyes observe construction and equipment, and to note signs of wear or deterioration, so that these may be corrected. For these reasons, safety inspections are essential.

Consulting Services

Our staff specializes in working with groups and organizations in helping design and/or help implement a variety of team building experiences. Prior to all events, a comprehensive needs assessment is completed. Group experiences include all levels of team building and are tailored to meet the identified needs of a group.

Team building experiences include: initiatives, low and high Ropes Course, weekend retreats or expeditions, and Myers Briggs Type Indicator administration and interpretation by qualified personnel. Our staff is available to travel to your site and conduct these programs.

Game Bag

A comprehensive bag of props for numerous games and initiatives. Cornerstone Design, Inc. will be happy to provide a complete list and prices which include shipping.

Ropes Course Manual

We encourage your comments and suggestions about this manual. Your input will assist us in our continuous effort to improve our services.

CHALLENGE
COURSE
KEEP OFF!

NOT to be used
without supervision by
authorized personnel.

NO TRESPASSING
ROPES COURSE

- Not to be used
without Supervision
by Authorized Personnel

NO
TRESPASSING

CHALLENGE
COURSE

To Be Used Only
Under Supervision
Of Authorized Personnel

NO
TRESPASSING
ROPES COURSE NOT TO BE
USED WITHOUT SUPERVISION
BY AUTHORIZED PERSONNEL

WARNING
UNAUTHORIZED
AND
UNSUPERVISED USE
—OF THE—
ROPES COURSE
IS UNSAFE
& PROHIBITED

PENALTY FOR
UNAUTHORIZED USE

NO FUTURE USE
OF THIS
FACILITY

Warning

The Complete Ropes Course Manual activities should not be attempted without proper training, or without proper supervision by trained and qualified professionals. Wrongful use of these activities or facilitating them without proper training may result in serious injury. This manual has been produced and designed to be used only by trained individuals.

Any liability for loss or damage, direct or consequential to the reader or to others, resulting from the use of the materials contained herein, whether such loss or damage results from errors, omissions, ambiguities, or inaccuracies in the materials contained herein or otherwise, are assumed by neither the author, publisher, seller, nor any distributor of this publication.

No warranties, expressed or implied, as to merchantability are intended to arise out of the sale or distribution of this publication, and this publication is sold "as is" and "with all faults." The liability of the author, publisher, seller, or any distributor of this publication on account of any such errors, omissions or ambiguities, shall in any event, be limited only to the price of this publication.

Contents

Appendix II

Preface

This guide is intended to serve as a checklist of procedures, techniques, and responsibilities for Ropes Course facilitators. The care and safety of participants is primary, and these factors must remain foremost in the mind of each individual working on the course. Facilitators must assist in successfully accomplishing any educational or personal goals the group has developed. Equally important is undertaking the tasks which include the upkeep of the physical course itself, inspecting structures regularly, and maintaining safety equipment.

Throughout the many operational activities which range from office to classroom to maintenance, this guide will "hold its own" as a useful resource, and should be within easy access of facilitators at all times. Even "experts" should be wise enough to keep a Ropes Course manual close at hand.

In order to maintain a high standard of professionalism and safety, facilitators refresh themselves on key points before or during each day of work. Development of "expert" skills is guaranteed when careful preparation and evaluation are a regular part of the daily schedule.

This Ropes Course manual does not have all the answers, yet it will serve as a broad-based guideline. It is designed as an aid to ensure that the basics are covered. It should be read by every staff person, regardless of their position, and preferably each individual should have his/her own copy. Facilitators can keep notes on the blank pages and margins provided to record observations, favorite techniques, and innovative ideas that add to safe and effective operation of the course.

Outdoor experiential education and Ropes Courses offer exciting and growing opportunities. Continue to increase a base of knowledge by reading books and periodicals, seeking out additional training, and communicating with others in the field.

Together we will continue to "fine tune" the Ropes Course. We will enjoy the simple beauty and perceived risk of its educational process which empowers individuals to reach for maximum potential and inspires teams to work in the spirit of cooperation.

> *"If I never try anything, I never learn anything. If I never take a risk, I stay where I am."*
> Author unknown

Welcome to the Ropes Course. Enjoy the Risk!!!

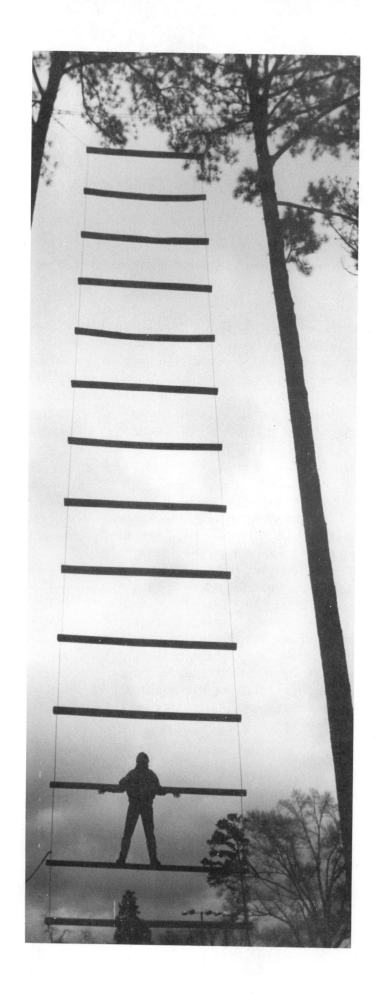

Acknowledgments

Any body of knowledge is shared as a result of the work of many individuals. Obviously, in the development of this manual there have been many contributors. We express our heartfelt thanks to those too many to mention, who have touched our lives and inspired us with the commitment to contribute to continued safe development of Outdoor Adventure Education.

Our gratitude and respect go to the pioneering work of Kurt Hahn and the many staff members, both past and present, of Outward Bound, Project Adventure, Inner Quest, Mike Fischesser of Alpine Tower, Bruce Smith of On Rope 1, and numerous others for their diligent efforts in promoting and carrying the torch for the Ropes Course industry.

Special thanks to those who contributed information, time, energy, and vision for this project: Scott Hager, Bobby Shaver, Diane Groff, Lee Gillis. Our appreciation goes out to those who assisted with editing tasks, Sylbie Yon, Kathleen Smith, Sam Sutcliffe, Brock Snyder and photographers Jay Moore and Dave Klim. Many thanks go out to John Scott for designing yet another wonderful book cover. Our thanks also go out to the many friends and our families who offered words of encouragement throughout the process of "birthing" this manual.

A small portion of the material in this publication was printed in a non-copyrighted document entitled Ropes Course Procedural Manual, written by Jim Wall, Cary Delano, and Bill Delano in 1990.

Chapter 1

Overview

Introduction to the Ropes Course

An Outdoor Challenge to the Mind, Body, and the Spirit

"Progress always involves risk; you can't steal second base and keep your foot on first." Fredrick Wilcox

The Challenge

The Ropes Course is an experiential adventure program which offers groups and individuals the opportunity to participate in a series of activities involving mental, physical, and emotional risk taking. The Ropes Course consists of an aesthetically designed series of ropes, cables, and logs combined in such a way as to simulate challenges that might be found in a natural setting. Safety and cooperation, as well as individual achievement, are essential to the program. These qualities are emphasized by trained instructors who guide groups through the course. The experience includes a variety of sessions planned around the various obstacles in order to examine and share common reactions, insights, and emotions such as joy, fear, fatigue, compassion, laughter, and love.

The Reward

Ropes Course programs offer participants an opportunity to increase their communication skills, while becoming effective at group problem-solving. Attempting and succeeding in these activities often gives one a feeling of accomplishment, self-worth, elation, and a recognition that seemingly impossible situations are in fact quite possible. Personal and professional situations may be simulated within a Ropes Course environment. While the real world hammers unsuccessful attempts, in a Ropes Course setting the exploration of solutions in a playful and non-threatening manner is commonplace.

Notes

Goals

The following basic goals should be included:

- Have safe fun!
- Attempt to work as a team.
- Take care of yourself and others.
- "Stretch" personally beyond known limits.
- Be respectful of others, always recognizing individual differences.

Figure 1-1. Having fun on the Running Zip!

Standards

Standards for the given group should be discussed early in the program in a respectful and appropriate manner for the given group. It is important that an individual participate by his/her own choice, rather than to please someone else. Without belaboring the point, request and confirm "agreement" to the following by a show of hands, an "aye!" (or any simple response of choice):

- Attendance for all scheduled portions of the program.
- No use of alcohol or non-prescription drugs.
- Commitment to stretch and develop in new ways.
- Support one another—when solicited, offer appropriate feedback.

Ropes Course History

Origin

Ropes Courses have been in existence in the United States since the early 1960s. However, they are still new to some areas of the country. According to Alan Hale, Director of the National Safety Network, Ropes Courses in America originated within the Outward Bound movement.

The initial course was constructed in Colorado at the first U.S. Outward Bound school. By today's standards the original course was very primitive. It was patterned after the military obstacle course, and a similar prototype developed in Europe, by Outward Bound founder, Kurt Hahn. It was built primarily with hemp rope, which deteriorated quickly. Belay systems were minimal, or nonexistent.

Evolution

There have been many changes since those early days. Today's Ropes Course utilizes a variety of safety systems, with elaborate safeguards engineered to protect participants from injury. Construction methods have also improved, with building materials and methods regularly updated. Steel aircraft cable and other specially designed hardware have replaced hemp and manila rope, making the modern Ropes Course safe and durable.

One significant development that has occurred throughout the past decade has been the use of utility poles in the construction of Ropes Courses. This development allows greater latitude in site construction due to the builder not being dependent on tree availability.

The original Ropes Courses were designed and built to enhance physical capabilities (agility, balance, and coordination); whereas today's courses address problem-solving skills, as well as individual and group dynamics issues.

Initially Used in Physical Education

In 1971, Project Adventure's first course was built in Massachusetts at Hamilton-Wenham Regional High School by Karl Rohnke and a band of conscripted high school sophomores. This was the beginning of a trend to integrate Ropes Courses into many types of programs. Their initial use in physical education classes has since extended to a broad range of applications in education, recreation, therapy, and organizational development.

Youth at Risk

Since the beginning, those who developed *youth at risk* programs have recognized the value of the Ropes Course experience. During the last decade, there has been a large movement by therapeutic agencies, substance abuse centers, and psychiatric hospitals to incorporate Ropes Courses into their offerings. Now, many outdoor educational centers, colleges, universities, camps, and hospitals are providing Ropes Course experiences as a major component of their programs.

Corporate Use of Ropes Courses

During the middle 1980s, the corporate world began turning to innovative firms that creatively use the Ropes Course to assist their executives in solving key organizational issues, and to create an environment for increased productivity and team work. Some specific professional development themes addressed include: team building, communication and problem-solving skills, risk-taking strategies, and stress reduction.

The Future

The future looks bright for Ropes Courses throughout the 1990s and the next decade. Because of these current trends in their usage and since measurable results are produced, it is safe to say that they will soon be adapted for virtually every type of select population.

The Ropes Course industry has taken a significant step recently in the formation of the Association of Challenge Course Technology (A.C.C.T.). A.C.C.T. was formed by a group of Ropes Course builders with the purpose of investigating current practices within the Ropes Course industry. The association has now formally adopted a set of standards for Ropes Course construction. The development of these standards, combined with the new program accreditation process by the Association for Experiential Education (AEE), has ensured that Ropes Courses will continue to be a viable, safe, and significant part of Adventure Education programs.

Indoor Ropes Courses

One year after Project Adventure began operation in 1971, Newburyport High School gave us a call wondering what we could do for them that would extend the use of their indoor space during the winter months. Responding in a way that was somewhat typical of our "what's next" modus operandi, we began doing what we did best, adventurously winging it in a casually competent manner.

Everyone in the New England area recognizes that Ropes Course activities are limited by the winter temperatures. This became an opportunity to find out, first hand, how some of the events could be adapted to fit into a gymnasium AND be fitted in such a way that the course materials could be pulled, slid, pushed or maneuvered out of the way so that the basketball coach wouldn't flip out.

Since then almost all of the low and high elements on a Ropes Course have been installed indoors. Admittedly some indoor spaces and unique construction areas have allowed more creative use of space. But in most cases, if it can be built outdoors between trees, it can also be installed indoors. Examples: Dangle Duo, Zip Wire, Two Line Bridge, Tension Traverse, Wild Woozey, Single Line Potpourri, All Aboard, Spider's Web, Mohawk Walk, Fidget Ladder, Pamper Plank, etc.

Karl's Historical Perspective

While talking with Jim Wall and Catherine Tait about different sections of this manual, we spent some time reminiscing about personal times we had spent on Ropes Courses. The conversation eventually segued to historical vignettes and ". . . where did this or that come from?" I found myself answering many of their questions about the actual history of an event ("Where did it come from?" "How was it named?"). They both suggested that other people might be interested in this esoteric Ropes Course trivia. So here's a few funambulating facts from somebody who was there.

All Aboard—I remember using this low element at The North Carolina Outward Bound School in 1968. At the time the 18 inch high platform was bolted to the top of four buried posts. When I eventually assumed responsibility for building the first course for Project Adventure (Hamilton-Wenham Regional High School, 1971), I took the basic idea, and arbitrarily established 2' x 2' as the "official" size, made it portable by nailing boards to the top of two parallel 4 x 4's, and named it the *All Aboard*, because that's what it was!

Seagull Landing—I've always liked swinging events. I suppose because I know that's what people like to do. (Check out how many back yards across this continent have swings of some sort hanging from a tree limb.) The Seagull Landing event developed serendipitously as I was trying to work on another swinging event. I had miscalculated the arc of a particular swing, and I found that the swinger was coming in much too fast toward the destination that I had in mind. Rather than taking the whole thing down, I played with it for awhile and I found that it was even more challenging, exciting, and fun (a hard to beat combination) to land on the destination stump on the return portion of the swing's arc. I felt very much like a seagull landing on a dock piling, so . . .

Wild Woozey—Peter Bryant told me about this event during a bus ride out of Denver. He even related the name at that time. We were on our way to the second annual AEE National Conference in Estes Park. That's it, that's all I know . . . except that I've built lots of them.

Mohawk Walk—We (PA staff) were on the final day of an adventure programming workshop for Project Adventure. On the last day, we used to offer some hands-on Ropes Course construction time so that people would have a better idea of what went into planning and building an element. I had the idea of taking a portable event called the *Sky Walk* and making it more permanent by using cables instead of rope. After completing the work (we were at Triton Regional High School in Byfield, MA), I asked the group to help name the event. Two of the participants were from the Kanawaukee Survival School in Canada. They said, "Why not name it after our tribe, we're a minority group and no one ever gives us much credit." So it became known as the *Mohawk Walk*.

Flying Squirrel—I was about 45 feet above the ground, sawing off the jagged end of a dead oak limb in anticipation of creating a high ropes element that seemed simple but needed. I was about half way through the limb when what seemed to be a large leaf detached from the end of the limb and began falling. The "leaf" fell about ten feet then radically changed direction, and, it did this again before it hit the ground *and ran away*. Unintentionally, I had disturbed the afternoon nap of a seldom seen nocturnal animal, a flying squirrel. The name was too appropriate to pass up.

Fidget Ladder—I had nothing to do with the concept of this very difficult low event, having experienced my first one at The Hurricane Outward Bound School in Maine. That one was fabricated of cable and pipes. Because I didn't know any better, this type of construction made a lot of sense. I started building them for Project Adventure in the early '70s using a rope ladder construction technique that I picked up in a knot book authored by a fellow named Rauol Graumont. Most Fidget Ladders measure 19 feet long, at least the ones supplied by PA, and that's because the first ones I made just happened to measure 19 feet. I called it a *Fidget Ladder* because that's what it did.

Rufus Little (former OB and PA employee and friend) and I used to make Fidget Ladders together in the basement of the *Iron Rail* (The name of PA's office in Hamilton, MA). Our fabricating techniques were still fairly primitive back then, as we depended almost entirely on hand (no power) labor. The rungs of the ladder all had to be grooved on the ends with a file, an arduous and terminally boring task. I suggested to Rufe that we do the grooving with a chain saw, and he agreed. (There weren't many committees to deal with at the time.) He held the dowels and I applied the growling chain to their tips with a deft touch, at least what I considered to be a deft touch. This all occurred indoors because it was so cold outdoors. One day, I had inadvertently mixed too much oil with the gas. As we continued grooving the dowels (that's a euphemism for the splintering, dowel jerking application of chain to wood), the room and our lungs quickly filled with a miasmic cloud of billowing chain saw exhaust. During a head-out-the-window break, Rufe asked why he didn't get to hold the chain saw rather than attempting to control the bucking dowels. I answered confidently (cough, cough . . .), "because it's my saw." That was well before *Challenge by Choice*.

Spider's Web—About 15 years ago I was writing and editing a publication called *Bag of Tricks*. Part of the content of that quarterly was adventure oriented material that readers shared with me. One reader mailed two poorly composed and slightly out of focus photos of a person being passed through what looked like a ragged spider web. Not too impressive, so I filed the photos and the brief description. A couple years later, what I had for publication was a bit weak so I looked through my files, pulled out the Spider Web info, edited the raw material, and the rest is adventure programming history. The Spider Web has become one of the most popular initiative problems *ever*. So much for my keen sense of programmatic functionality, and I would like to give my sincere thanks to John Jarboe who shared that information so many years ago.

Pamper Pole—This is the best! I have been most pleased with this nutsy notion over the years than with any of the other ideas I've originated. There's a detailed write-up about this high Ropes Course element in Volume 2 of FUNN STUFF, but for now, here's where the name came from.

About two years after we started using the Pamper Pole, a woman, standing on top of the pole lost control of the sphincter muscle controlling fluid output, a not so unusual medical phenomenon stimulated by fear, emotion, etc. This slight slip of the sphincter might have gone unnoticed save for the revealing characteristic of her khaki pants. She good-naturedly said, "I should have been wearing *Pampers*."

There's more, but we have a lot of material to cover in the following pages, and it's time to get to it. Thanks for joining me in this brief nostalgic review, it has been fun—it's always fun.

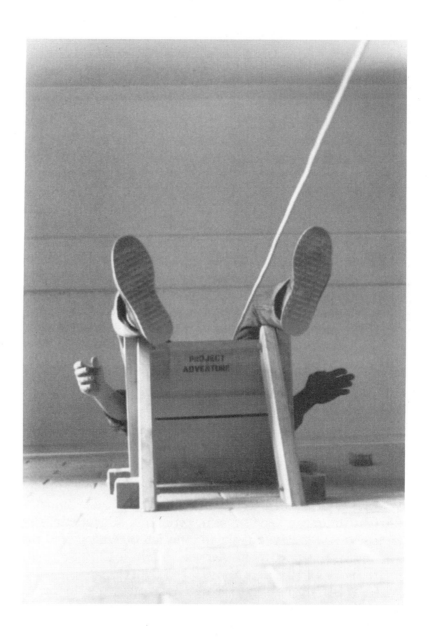

Staff Training

The following basic and advanced level requirements are provided as a guideline for Staff Training. Each course director should use these when establishing his/her requirements.

Basic Facilitator Requirements

Requires a minimum of 40 hours training in Ropes Course facilitation. Outside training must be approved by the director.

A basic facilitator must have knowledge of and demonstrate proficiency in the following:

- Successful completion of CPR and Standard First Aid training.
- Ability to quickly and confidently tie all necessary knots.
- Capability to set up and take down each event.
- Ability to present and understand each event, including all safety issues and features.
- Use and understand group dynamic facilitation skills as they apply to a Ropes Course.
- Ability to prepare (front-loading) and follow-up (debriefing) for the group.
- Knowledge of the use of the experiential learning cycle.
- Working knowledge of equipment.

Advanced Facilitator Requirements/Lead Facilitator

- Obtain Basic Facilitator status.
- Current CPR and Standard First Aid.
- Minimum 80 hours working as a basic facilitator.
- Receive course director's approval by successful completion of a written evaluation, demonstration of skills, and face-to-face interview.
- Successfully demonstrate a high course rescue.
- Ability to conduct a pre-meeting of participants.
- Ability to appropriately review and interpret medical forms.
- Superior working knowledge of all safety gear used on a Ropes Course.
- Ability to develop a schedule that will address the group's issues and goals.

Maintaining Advanced Facilitator Status

- Work with at least two different facilitators per year.
- Facilitate a minimum of one group per month. (This guideline may be influenced by the experience level of the facilitator.)
- To regain advanced status, a person must work with an Advanced Facilitator for a minimum of three days and receive his/her approval. In addition, s/he must have a face-to-face interview with course director.

Operational Guidelines

Staff—Participant Ratio

Every Ropes Course should be evaluated for the number of participants that it can comfortably accommodate on the course itself, and at entrance and exit points (considering time requirements for each). An estimation can then be made for maximum capacity. The number of facilitators required will be somewhat dependent on the size and idiosyncrasies of the course and emergency requirements. Basic guidelines are as follows:

- Participants: minimum of ten, maximum of 20 in one group on either high or low course. A larger group may be divided into smaller groups, i.e. 80 into four groups of 20.
- Staff: regardless of the type of high course there must always be two facilitators. The following ratios should by used to determine the additional number of facilitators based on group size.

Static High Course
(3 minimum)   *1 facilitator / 7 participants*
Dynamic High Course
(2 minimum)   *1 facilitator / 10 participants*

- Low course staff: regardless of the size of group there should be at least two facilitators. If you have a small group the second facilitator could be someone less trained yet able to handle logistics and assist in emergencies. A 1:10 ratio can be used to determine the number of staff. Example: a group of 20 could be divided into two groups of ten for certain games or elements requiring only one facilitator per group, then both groups could come back together as a group of 20 with two facilitators.

Participant Requirements

- All participants should attend some form of preparation meeting prior to any scheduled event.
- Age minimum varies from course to course. Young children, based upon the child's maturity level, may participate in structured activities requiring individual adult assistance, with permission from course director.

All participants, age 18 and under, must have a parent or guardian sign a release form for both the high and low courses.

- **All participants must have signed and dated required forms:**

    Informed Consent
    Medical Information and Authorization Form
    Assumption of Risk/Voluntary Release

- Participants must be properly fitted with safety equipment and educated in its use.
- A buddy system should be used with a belay system on a static course, so that participants on the high course each have a partner at all times.
- Participants must be on belay while climbing from the ground to high course level.
- All participants should be actively involved in a follow-up contact after the program.

The above staff and participant recommendations are offered as a guide only. You will surely adapt these guidelines and add to them in order to develop your own course policies.

Chapter 2

Safety and Equipment

General Safety

In the Beginning . . . Set the Stage for Safety

It is important to set the stage for safety from the first interaction with participants. You may begin this process by contracting with the group to agree to all goals and standards at the first preparation meeting and also at the beginning of each day on the course.

Staff who start out with a clear commitment from the participants prepare the way for a smooth and safe day. This cannot be emphasized enough! Take your time discussing what the group is trying to achieve; after all, isn't this the reason why they are here?

Deal Promptly with Deviation from the Commitment

Stop the action if necessary, and deal with the situation so that peer reaction and feedback work for you. Take care to confront any deviation in a straight forward manner, clarifying difficulties, but without assigning guilt.

You are in the position of enforcing course standards, so remind people of their commitment if problems develop. You can call an end to the day at any time because of continued safety violations. You are in charge!

Spotting and Safe Problem Solving Require Critical Focus

Keeping your senses focused sharply on the action and its surrounding environment will attune you to potential and actual dangers.

Your responsibility is to anticipate potential accidents and to stop the wrong actions before they escalate. Make your reasons for halting the action clear, then demonstrate the proper way to perform the activity. This does not mean solving the problem for participants. Proceed when the participants understand, and they have shown renewed commitment to a safe approach.

Notes

Use a Methodical Approach

Simpler exercises lead toward more complicated ones. Trust, communication, and correct spotting techniques need to be established before moving on to more advanced activities.

You are Responsible for Taking Care of Any Accident That Occurs

Halt the action at any time to correct dangerous practices. The majority of accidents occur on low elements, games, or from tripping over roots while walking from one event to another. Check trails and walking areas on the course for these avoidable hazards. Develop and practice an emergency plan.

All staff should be trained annually in standard first aid and CPR.

A first aid kit should be available on the course at all times of operation.

If an injury does occur, stop the activity immediately. Keep the victim calm and still. Have staff members keep the other participants at a distance unless they are needed. Evacuate the course if necessary. Implement "EMERGENCY PROCEDURES."

Emotional outbursts are not uncommon. Facilitators should be ready to offer a hand or shoulder to lean on when appropriate. Offering comfort and positive words are key factors for controlling emotional situations. Let the group help you give support before continuing.

Double Check All Elements Before Use

You are responsible for testing the safety and integrity of all activities before they are used by participants. You could possibly be considered legally negligent if an accident occurs involving safety gear or structures that should have been checked regularly.

Instruct with a Relaxed, Non-competitive Attitude

You should clearly and calmly cover all the technical and operational information that the students *need to know*. Don't tell "war stories" just to impress the group or make yourself seem important. Be casually competent, not overbearingly officious.

Spotting

What Does Spotting Mean?

Spotting is actively safeguarding the movements of another participant. Spotting usually involves several participants or "spotters" protecting a "climber," who may be at a position ground level to six feet off the ground. The primary duty of a spotter is to support and protect the head and upper body area of a climber in case a fall should occur. Falls above five to six feet can be devastating to both the faller and spotter alike. Spot accurately.

Rules of Spotting

Two basic rules of correct spotting are:

- Attention: the spotter watches the climber constantly.
- Anticipation: the spotter's hands extend toward the climber.

Beyond these two rules, spotting varies considerably according to both the event and the highly variable positions of the climber. Spotters must be instructed to anticipate the next movement of the climber. The spotter should be close to the climber, but s/he should not make physical contact unless a fall occurs.

It is important that the climber trust his/her spotter(s). It's also important for spotters to be comfortable with the responsibility of their position. Spotting techniques must be taught and practiced at the beginning of Day One, after warm-ups, and reviewed after warm-ups on Day Two. This practice will insure confidence and trust on both sides, as each participant takes his/ her turn participating and spotting.

Spotting Enhances Team Building

Good spotting is one of the most useful team-building aspects on the Ropes Course. Each participant in turn assumes responsibility for the well-being of another participant during each event. Having done so, a good measure of trust develops among group members. Individual confidence is also heightened in this supportive atmosphere.

Number and Placement of Spotters

As a facilitator, you must accurately estimate the optimum number and placement of spotters for each event. Encourage your group to figure this out for themselves as a problem-solving experience, while assisting with verbal observations and hints.

However, it is your responsibility to ultimately maneuver the group into optimum placement, prior to the climber's ascent, and to see to it that the group maintains optimum attention and remains at said agreed place. The facilitator should know the best spotting techniques to be used for each event and for the various positions required. Also, the facilitator should understand why these techniques and positions are better than others and insist that your group use them.

Most events should be safeguarded by five or six spotters. This means that five or six members out of a group of twelve are actively involved at any

Notes

time. As a facilitator, you should encourage the "spotting crew" to change with each new climber. Otherwise, you can expect the non-spotters to feel uninvolved, and/or the spotters to become tired and feel over used.

Don't let your "first to volunteer" spotters burn out. Twenty minutes of active spotting can leave upraised arms drained of blood, shoulders aching, and nerves a bit frayed. Get the group to devise its own "rotation system." Keep everyone involved. As facilitator the challenge is to ensure optimum spotting by "fresh" participants at all times. This should be accomplished without being overbearing in your approach.

Facilitator's Responsibility

As a facilitator, devote your attention to making certain that your clients spot well, rather than becoming a spotter yourself. An exception to this procedure is during times of demonstration.

Always Use Commands

Before any spotting occurs make certain that all participants go through the spotting commands:

Participant asks, "Spotters ready?"

All spotters respond, "Ready!"

Participant then states what s/he is about to do, i.e. "climbing," "trusting," "falling."

All spotters respond by answering what the participant is about to do, i.e. "climb away," "trust away," "fall away."

Lifting

After teaching the basics of spotting, allow the group to use their newly acquired skills toward creating a "safety-net" during the lifting instructions.

"Lifting" in this context is the acceptable means of assisting a climber to gain additional height to perform an event (such as The Wall). This procedure employs a climber, a lifter, and three spotters.

The lifter should stand erect, back straight, with knees locked, fingers interlocked, palms up, and arms straight. The climber steps up into the lifter's clasped hands, grasps the lifter's shoulders firmly, and is then lifted onto the event.

Meanwhile, two spotters stand behind the climber with arms outstretched toward his/her shoulder blades. A third spotter is back-to-back with the lifter, steadying him/her—unless, of course, the lifter is backed against a tree, wall, or some other fixture.

It is important that lifting be done primarily using the skeletal system, rather than just the muscles, or a sprain/strain may result. Of primary importance is the proper orientation of the back—it must be straight. A bent-over lifter tends to raise the climber using only back muscles (a mistake that can result in back injury). The greater risk in lifting is to the lifter. The last thing to be checked by the facilitator before a lift is performed is the straightness of the lifter's back, i.e. his/her erect posture while lifting.

Always ask, prior to teaching the lift, whether there are any "bad" backs or knees in the group. Suggest that anyone with a "problem back" or "athlete's knee" not be part of the lifting crew.

Lifting, like spotting, is a useful group interaction device. Performed properly, it is a safe procedure. Teach it well, and emphasize that students follow safe and appropriate procedures.

Belaying

Belaying is a technique which protects a climber by use of ropes, carabiners, cable, and belay devices. A rope is attached to the climber, which then runs between the safety cable and the belayer. The belayer will hold the rope in such a way that s/he is able to catch and keep the climber safe if s/he should fall.

Belay Systems

Belay systems are either dynamic or static, or a combination of the two.

Dynamic Belay utilizes a belayer who controls the safety rope to the participant. The belayer is stationed on the ground and is able to protect, catch, or lower the participant in a safe and controlled manner. The belayer can use a belaying device such as a sticht plate to aid and assist in controlling friction. A less typical means of dynamic belay, yet still acceptable, is the standing hip (body) belay. This procedure utilizes the belayer's body to provide friction.

Static Belay or self-belay is a system that connects a participant to an overhead belay cable by use of a carabiner and a three to six foot piece of rope or webbing attached to the climber's harness. This system is put into use after a participant has been dynamically belayed to a high element.

Australian Back-up Belay—acting as the belayer, tie on a Swiss seat arrangement, Studebaker wrap, or step into a commercial harness. Using a bowline-on-a-bight in the end of the belayer's end of the rope (imagine a bottom belay situation on a Burma Bridge), clip the formed loops into the front of the two harnesses with locking carabiners. Here comes the simple part. As the climber climbs, the belayers back up and continue backing up until the climber reaches his/her goal, in this case the foot cables of the Burma Bridge. If the climber falls, the belayers literally do nothing, except eventually walk forward to let the climber smoothly down. There is nothing to let go of and no rope movement to burn exposed skin. So, where's the mystique? It's all gone—in this case replaced by pure function.

Problems? Contraindications? A couple.

1. If the climber is much heavier (over 50 pounds) than the two belayers, clip the two loops of an additional bowline-on-a-bight, at the end of the belay line, into two additional side-by-side "back-up" belayers, for a total of four belayers.
2. The belayer must have an obstacle-free back-up path to follow for the length of the belay. This technique does not work if the climber plans to move laterally on an element, e.g. across a Two Line Bridge; well . . . maybe on a telephone pole course in the middle of a field, but not amidst a stand of trees. Beware the clear-cut mentality.
3. After the belay "catch" is made and lowering begins, there is a natural tendency to be pulled forward at a pace which is faster than a walk. Simply be aware of this and control your forward speed by leaning back. Belayers should keep one leg forward at all times.
4. If the belay is a long one (over 200 feet) supply the belayer with an ice ax on frosty days. That's a joke—I say, *that's a joke, son!*

So, if your problem is how to safely train enough belayers for use with additional students on high Ropes Course elements, try the Australian back-up belay. It works "down under."

A Static Ropes Course consists of a series of connected elements. A participant traverses from element to element by use of a static belay system. In contrast, a dynamic Ropes Course involves largely separate elements from which a participant is dynamically belayed.

Belaying is an essential skill that should be taught by a professional and practiced regularly by facilitators. The information and photographs in this manual are intended for review by trained individuals and are not intended to be instructional.

Terminology of Belaying

Belayer—Person at the end of the rope who protects, catches, or lowers a climber.

Walking Belay—A belay system that moves with the climber from Point A to Point B.

Anchor Point—A fixed point to attach the belayer or belay device.

Fixed Belay—A belay point that is stationary and does not move from point to point.

Brake Hand—After rope passes around the body or through a belay device, it is held by this hand. This is generally the stronger hand. **The brake hand never leaves the dominant rope.**

Guide Hand—On the side of the rope going to the climber, this hand aids in taking in and letting out the rope. At other times, it is used for rope tension. The guide hand does not assist in the braking sequence.

Commands Used in Climbing and Belaying

Commands should be used and mastered in belay *practice*, so that they are automatic during climbing situations. **The belayer maintains voice and eye contact with climber at all times.** The following standard climbing commands should be learned and implemented during all events which include belayed climbing.

Climber — when clipped in	"On Belay"
Belayer — when ready, acknowledging	"Belay On"
Climber — ready to climb	"Climbing"
Belayer — tells climber to go on	"Climb On"
Climber — if rope is too tight	"Slack"
Belayer — responds with 6 inches of slack rope to each command until climber is satisfied or safety is compromised.	
Climber — if rope too loose	"Up Rope"
Belayer — takes up slack	

Climber — when off belay   **"Off Belay"**
Belayer — *only then* lets go of rope   **"Belay Off"**

Belaying Techniques

The following techniques for dynamic belaying are applicable for use with either body or belaying devices. The belay system utilizes a shear reduction pulley.

- Use proper belay commands.
- Keep brake hand on the rope at **ALL** times.
- Assign a participant the job of keeping rope in rope bag.
- Stand close to the element, but not directly beneath the climber.
- Use both hands equally while retrieving the belay rope.
- Maintain eye and voice contact with climber at all times.
- Always keep appropriate tension on the belay rope.
- Remember the belay rope is there only to protect the climber in case of a fall, not to assist the climber.
- Stay aligned with a laterally moving climber.
- If weight difference is of concern, assign a participant to stand behind and hold belayer's harness to act as a dynamic anchor.
- Don't let climber get ahead of belayer's ability to take up slack or let out rope. Talk to one another.
- If you chose to use gloves, wear properly fitted leather palm gloves.
- Always lower participants in a controlled manner.
- Check participants harness and carabiners before the climb.

Practice, practice, practice.

When time permits and it is appropriate to the goals of the group, you may want to allow participants to belay each other. A facilitator should serve as a back-up belayer in this case.

Belaying Positions

Figure 2-1. Non-fixed anchored belay position.

Figure 2-2. Fixed anchored belay.

Notes

Belaying Sequences

Figure 2-3. Step 1. Hand positioning indicates start of belay sequence. (All illustrations show arms extended for clarity; in actual use the elbows display a greater bend.)

START

Figure 2-4. Step 2. While gripping the rope the left hand is pulled in and the right hand extends.

Figure 2-5. Step 3. The left hand slides up the rope and grips both ropes *above* the right (brake) hand.

Notes

Figure 2-6. Step 4. The right (brake) hand slides down the rope toward the belayer's body.

Figure 2-7. Step 5. As the right hand establishes itself in the start position (above) the left hand releases the braking section of rope. The belayer is then ready to repeat the sequence.

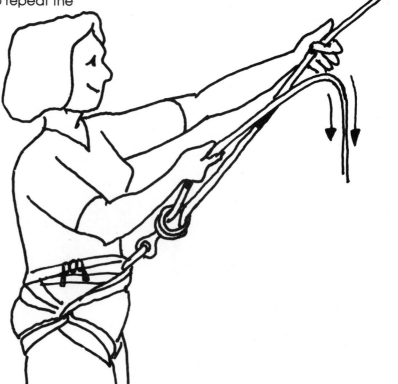

Equipment

Ropes

Kernmantle: a core covered rope. The core (parallel twisted nylon fibers) is the kern. The mantle is the woven covering. This specialty rope is used in two different sizes, 11 millimeter and nine millimeter. The 11 millimeter is used for belaying, and the nine millimeter is used for tying seat harnesses. Tensile strength for nine millimeter rope is 3,800 pounds and for the 11 millimeter is 5,500 pounds.

Twisted: a three-strand hawser laid rope. This rope is a polyester and polypropylene blend. It is generally used for fabricating crab claws (a self-belaying system on a static course), a zip rope connector, and in some cases a belay rope (Pamper Pole). A twisted rope is less expensive and more resistant to wear. Bowline tensile strength is approximately 3,500 pounds.

Kernmantle and/or twisted rope can be manufactured as either dynamic or static rope. A dynamic rope stretches and it is used in belaying situations. A static rope has very little stretch, and it is used under load in rescue situations.

Skills—Know how to:

- Coil rope properly for storage.
- Remove kinks.
- Butterfly coil for handling or throwing.
- Tie knots as suggested in this manual.
- Inspect rope regularly for fluffs, cuts, or breaks.
- Tie a Studebaker wrap or Swiss seat harness.

Figure 2-8.
Kernmantle rope (right) and twisted rope.

Webbing

One inch tubular nylon webbing

This "hollow" nylon webbing is used to make seat harnesses, girth hitches on anchor points, crab claws and static lines. Tensile strength measures at 4,000 pounds.

Skills—Know how to:

- Tie a Studebaker wrap using a square knot and double overhand in the tails as a finishing sequence.
- Tie slings and girth hitches in the webbing using water knots.
- Inspect webbing for unraveling and stitch integrity.

Figure 2-9. Tubular webbing.

Harnesses

Harnesses are either commercially made or tied by the student using nine millimeter rope or one inch tubular webbing. A Swiss seat arrangement or Studebaker wrap is the most commonly tied harness.

Skills—Know how to:

- Put on and adjust a commercial seat harness.
- Inspect a seat harness for wear.
- Tie a Swiss seat or Studebaker wrap (see page 70 for illustration).

Figure 2-10.
Adjustable commercial harnesses.

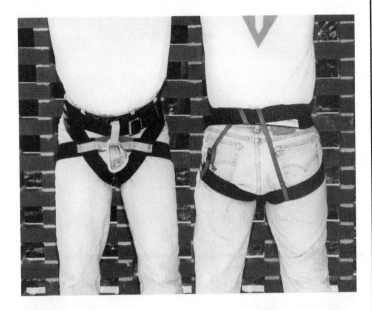

Figure 2-11.
Sized commercial harness.

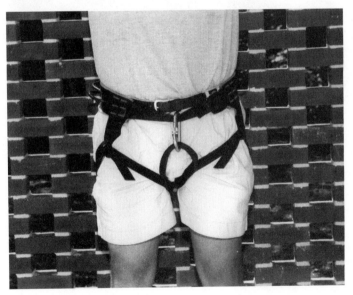

Chest Harnesses

A commercially made non-adjustable harness (S, M, L, XL) that protects the chest of the participant. Must be used in conjunction with a seat harness.

Skills—Know how to:

- Put on harness and adjust it.
- Inspect for wear.
- Use in conjunction with a Studebaker wrap.

Figure 2-12. Adjustable commercial harness and chest harness.

Full Body Harnesses

A full body harness is generally a commercially made, one piece adjustable harness that encompasses the body and distributes the fall forces throughout the torso.

Skills—Know how to:
- Put on a full body harness and adjust it.
- Inspect the body harness for wear.

Figure 2-13.
Full body harness, front.

Notes

Figure 2-14.
Full body harness, rear.

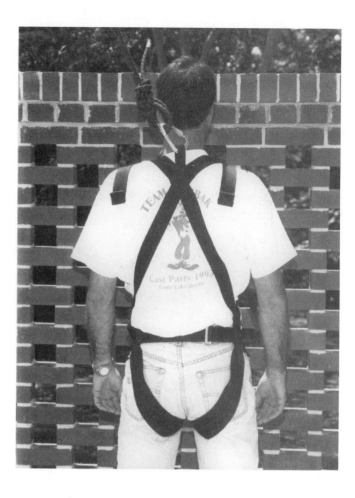

Carabiners

Carabiners are spring activated, impressively strong, metal links used to connect the climbing rope to a harness system. Each carabiner has a gate. Gates should be opened out and away from the webbing or rope connection. Carabiners either have a gate locking system or they don't.

Locking carabiners are required in ALL belay systems. (Note: If you always use locking carabiners you will eliminate the safety hazard of using a non-locking carabiner that requires a locking situation—we suggest eliminating non-locking carabiners from your Ropes Course.)

Note: "If you don't screw down you are likely to screw up." This quaint quote refers to the climbing orientation of a carabiner or rapid link. The link orientation should always be such that the gate closes in the direction of gravity's pull.

1. **Locking "D" Steel Carabiners** are "D" shaped ("D" shaped carabiners are stronger than oval shaped ones), with locking screw gates or collars. Generally rated at 5,000 pounds tensile strength, these carabiners are used to clip onto a steel cable.

Figure 2-15. Steel locking carabiner.

2. **Locking "D" Aluminum Carabiners** are "D" shaped with locking collars. Generally rated at 6,000 pounds tensile strength, these carabiners are used for rope to rope, or rope to harness connections.

Figure 2-16. Aluminum locking carabiner.

Skills—Know how to:
- Clip carabiners into belay system.
- Clip carabiner to a seat harness.
- Check regularly for wear.
- Maintain.

Pulleys

Most programs currently use steel sheave pulleys on belay cables instead of carabiners. Pulleys that are designed solely for belay cable use can be purchased from several companies. Make sure, however, that they meet A.C.C.T. specifications.

1. A **Single Pulley** (with case hardened sheave) is used to connect a rope belay system to the belay cable. A pulley enables the belay system to roll freely along the cable.

Figure 2-17. Single cable pulleys.

2. A **Shear Reduction Pulley** (with aluminum sheave) is often used in conjunction with a single wheel pulley to connect the rope belay system to the belay cable. These pulleys are connected together by two half-inch rapid links or two steel carabiners. (Two carabiners are used to allow the SR pulley to pivot, orient the belay rope correctly, and to prevent cable-pulley cheeks from rubbing on the cable.) Project Adventure has developed a pulley/shear reduction combination device that only requires one rapid link.

Figure 2-18. Running dynamic system; with single cable pulley, two locking carabiners, and spin static pulley.

3. A **Zip Wire Pulley** is attached to the participant by using a locking steel carabiner and a double eye spliced section of 5/8 inch multiline.

Figure 2-19. Two-wheeled zip wire pulleys.

4. A **Shear Reduction Block** is a device that reduces shear on the belay rope. Commonly used on the Pamper Pole element, it is attached to the belay cable with two half-inch rapid links clipped together in a line. The block also has an integral back-up cable which is attached to the belay cable with a single half-inch rapid link.

Figure 2-20. Shear reduction block.

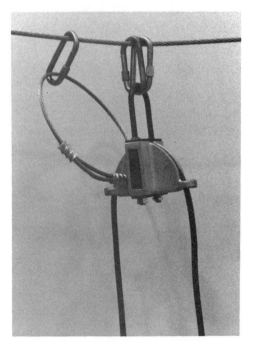

Skills—Know how to:
- Set up belay pulley on the belay cable.
- Determine when and how to use the various pulleys.
- Clean and inspect pulleys for wear.

Belay Devices

Belay devices are used to aid in belaying a participant. ATCs (Air Traffic Controllers), Sticht Plates, Tubers, and GriGris are the four most commonly used belay devices in a Ropes Course setting.

Skills—Know how to:

- Set up an ATC and Sticht plate.
- Inspect for wear.
- Determine when and how to use belay devices.

Figure 2-21. Belay devices: ATC, Sticht Plate, Tuber.

Figure 2-22. Belay device: GriGri.

Figure Eight Devices

Figure Eight devices are most often made of forged alloy and frequently anodized. They resemble the number eight. They are used for rappelling. They are *no* longer recommended for belaying because they tend to twist (pigtail the rope). One style of Figure Eight is the rescue figure eight which is used to perform rescues.

Skills—Know how to:

- To insert the rope properly.
- Know and understand the different types and usage.
- Know and understand the different methods and places to attach and use the Figure Eight for rescues.

Figure 2-23. Rescue Figure Eight.

Figure 2-24. Regular Figure Eight.

Rescue Blades

A "rescue blade" should be available at all times. Folding knives or straight knives are less preferred because of the chance of stabbing or cutting a participant. Folding knives are best used to cut rope on the ground. Scissors (EMT type) or a hook knife are the safest for cutting rope at height.

Figure 2-25. Rescue blades: utility scissors, open blade knife.

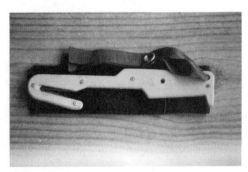

Figure 2-26. Rescue blade: rescue knife.

Helmets

Helmets are worn when rappelling, on climbing walls, and on all high events, and they help protect participants from head injuries.

Figure 2-27. Helmets.

Skills—Know how to:
- Properly fit a helmet to participant.
- Inspect helmet for wear.
- Maintain cleanliness.

Rope Bag

Rope bags are specifically designed to carry and store rope. They are usually equipped with shoulder straps and hanging loops. Attach a plastic pouch on the rope bag in which to store a rope log (record of use). Rope bags aid in rescues, in keeping the rope off the ground, and preclude U/V deterioration. See Rescue Chapter for a complete description of a Rescue Bag.

Notes

Figure 2-28.
Rope bag.

Gloves

Leather palm gloves protect the belayer's hands in case of a climber's fall. They are essential for use in a standing hip (body) belay and are recommended for use with a sticht plate.

Figure 2-29.
Leather-palmed gloves.

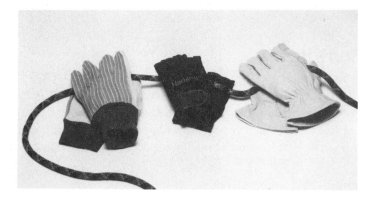

Care of Equipment

Ropes

Generally, kernmantle climbing rope has a shelf life of four to five years if it is stored in a cool, dry space. As nylon ages it loses strength over time. All UIAA 11 millimeter climbing rope is amazingly strong, much stronger than the human body itself. In order to help a rope last, there are some things you can do:

- Never step on a rope. Dirt can be ground through the mantle into the kern, cutting or weakening fibers over time. Dirt particles inside the rope grind against interior rope fibers and cut them. Do not allow nylon to rub against nylon under pressure, as this synthetic material has a low melting/burning point.

Figure 2-30. Which way is the course?

- Keep rope clean. If your rope gets very dirty, it can be washed on the gentle cycle in a machine with mild soap in cool water. Spaghetti it inside a cloth stuff-sack then put in the washing machine. Do not dry the rope in a clothes dryer. A commercial rope washer attached to a hose can help flush out dirt also. Air dry rope on a rack out of direct sunlight. Do not put a rope away wet! It can mildew.

Notes

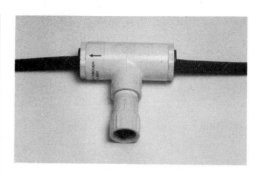

Figure 2-31. Rope washer.

- Under certain circumstances dirt may cut interior fibers.
- Do not store ropes on unpainted concrete. The base chemicals can leach from the concrete and cement and into the rope, which can weaken the fibers. Fumes from corrosives in a storage facility can eat at the fibers. Exposure to ultraviolet rays also weaken the sheath of the rope.
- Always untie knots when storing rope even if it is only overnight. Storing the rope free of kinks prevents the same fibers from repeatedly taking the weight load. AND, this will provide necessary practice to tie the knot the next day.
- The best method for storage is in a rope bag. The use of a rope bag keeps the rope from unnecessarily having contact with the ground.
- Use a belay rope only for belaying, not for tug of wars, laying out game boundaries or as tow ropes.
- Periodically check the rope by feeling along its length for unusual lumps or depressions. Either of these could indicate a kern problem which reduces the strength of the rope. A depression may mean severed strands inside. A lump means one or more strands inside the rope have become twisted. Was the rope passed over a Figure Eight under weight load too many times without unwinding it?
- Excessive fraying means that the rope needs to be discarded or have that section cut off. A constantly used kernmantle rope will become fuzzy. An excessive fray means the mantle is cut or ripped so that the core fibers are showing and/or sticking out. If a sheath wears through so that the kern is exposed, retire the rope. However, a hawser-laid rope can become so fuzzy so as to resemble a caterpillar but it can still be used safely.

Figure 2-32. Worn kernmantle rope.

- Keep your rope away from contaminates such as: charcoal lighter fluids, gas, or paint cans, and insect repellent. DEET can melt nylon.
- Rope ends should be neatly melted to alleviate problems with fraying (cowstails). "Touch" the taped and cut end of a rope with the pencil-like flame of a propane torch.

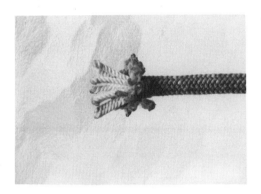

Figure 2-33. Non-melted rope end.

- If the core is showing at the end of the rope, or the sheath pulls beyond the core by a couple of inches, pulling firmly along the rope to slide the sheath towards the other end will sometimes adjust the sheath to its original position. If you can adjust the sheath, tape, cut and melt the rope. If you are not able to adjust the sheath to its original position, tape, cut and melt the end a few inches from the end. If more than a couple of inches are at fault, consult a qualified professional. Although unusual, there have been occasions when a sliding sheath has been the cause of retiring a rope, recycling it to a game bag as a jump rope.
- Identify each length of rope with a color-coded tag made of tape so that a log of usage may be kept. Keep the rope log attached to a similarly color-coded rope bag.

Webbing and Harnesses

Harnesses are made of nylon and have an age limit of four to five years. As with all manufactured equipment, you need to check with the manufacturer for specific details on age limits. Care for harnesses is similar to rope care since they are both made from the same material.

- Keep webbing and harnesses clean and dry. Use mild detergent for washing.

Notes

- Identify each piece of webbing and harness so that a usage log may be kept.
- There are three inspection areas to be aware of for harnesses, in addition to those mentioned in the rope section. They are: stitching, specific wear areas, and fraying.
- Stitching is the first noticeable part of a harness to weaken with age. It is possible to actually tear stitches on an old harness even though it may still be impossible to rip the actual webbing material by hand.

Figure 2-34. Harness with broken stitches.

- Remember, nylon rubbing or nylon running across nylon under pressure creates heat quickly, and both will melt the nylon with surprising speed.

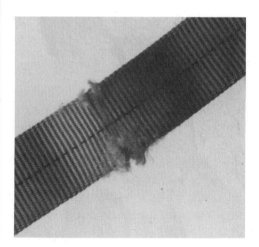

Figure 2-35. Worn tubular webbing.

Carabiners

- If the gate does not work smoothly or close completely, or if the locking barrel does not work smoothly, dirt may be in the hinge or corrosion may have occurred. Clean and lubricate the hinge. A silicone lubricant will not tend to attract dirt as readily as oil. Wipe off excess lubricant to prevent contamination of the ropes.
- Keep carabiners clean. Do not step on them or abuse them (such as dropping them from heights).
- Lubricate hinges (use non-oil lubricant) at the hinge point, when the gate becomes sticky. Remember to thoroughly wipe off excess lubricant before using the hinge again. Remove tree sap from the hinges with kerosene.

- Identify each piece of equipment with a tag made of tape, so that a usage log may be kept.
- Check integrity of the pins. If there is excessive side play in an open gate, or if the pins are pitted with rust, discard the carabiner immediately.
- Look for grooves on the inside of the carabiner caused by rope or cable indicating excessive wear. The type of wear is most often caused by running the carabiner over cable. This is often seen on carabiners that are used on static courses. Aluminum carabiners should *never* be run over cable. Retire all grooved carabiners.

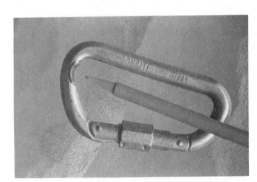

Figure 2-36. Worn aluminum carabiner.

- Do not drop carabiners on hard surfaces such as on rock or a gym floor. There is a possibility that a hidden, or internal crack could develop. Even a close examination may not detect a crack. An x-ray may be the only way to tell. If you do not have an x-ray machine at your disposal don't drop the carabiners!

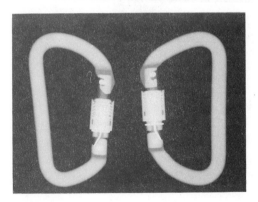

Figure 2-37. X-ray of carabiners in good condition.

Pulleys

Most Ropes Course pulleys do not need scheduled maintenance. Steel sheave pulleys used on belay cables are usually fitted with sealed bearings so lubricating is not necessary. Other types of pulleys, fitted with a brass bushing, may be lubricated if desired. Look at the wheels to see if there are grooves evident from the cable scoring the sheaves. If so, a new sheave can be installed *if* the side plates are in good condition. Avoid running an aluminum sheave pulley over a steel cable because this will quickly cause grooving of the wheel.

Avoid removing any axle nut that has a plastic washer built into it. The plastic is what acts as the locking mechanism keeping the nut in place. One or two times on or off is the limit before a new "aircraft nut" should be installed. Taking a pulley apart is not recommended. Call the manufacturer if there is a problem. Pulleys recommended for use on ropes courses are very strong, with tensile strengths rated at over 10,000 pounds.

- Care includes not dropping them on hard surfaces. Try not to slam the belay pulley against the serving sleeve. This action hammers dents into the side cheeks.
- If a pulley is left up on a course overnight with a lazy-line reeved through it, be sure to leave slack in the line if it is tied off to a tree. This prevents the pulley from slamming repeatedly into the serving sleeve as wind may cause a tensioning and draping of the cable. This also prevents dents and grooves in the side plates. If sharp edges result, the pulley should be retired.

Figure 2-38. Karl inspecting Shear Reduction Block.

- With shear reduction type pulleys, check to see if the holding pin, nut, and second bolt are in place before and during use. If a belay pulley has a back-up rapid link, check to see that it is closed tightly.
- On older pulleys, if the wheel is rubbing against and grooving the inside of the cheeks and slowing down the wheel's rotation, there may be a problem with either the bolt, side-plates, or wheel orientation. Whichever the case, if you are not satisfied with the pulley's performance, avoid the temptation of trying to fix it. In cases where a new sheath is needed, the pulley can be salvaged. Again, call the manufacturer if in doubt.
- Severe rust, which causes pits in the bolts, back-up rapid links, or holding pin, is cause for replacement of parts, or the entire unit.
- Lubricate all moving parts (non-oil lubricant). Then thoroughly wipe off excess lubricant before using them again. Do not attempt to lubricate sealed bearings.
- Identify each piece of equipment with an etching pen, so that a usage log may be kept.

Belay Devices and Figure Eights

There are a myriad of these devices on the market so that choosing one for your program can be confusing. These items do not require regular maintenance.

- Some of the most sophisticated devices, like a GriGri, have levers and cams. Keep the moving parts clean and free from debris. Read all the instructions which come with the new device. Usually included are important items of information, hints, and operating instructions.
- Care for belay devices should be the same as the care for carabiners. Do not drop onto hard surfaces or from heights. A sudden shock from a drop onto a rock may cause a crack in the metal which may not be apparent by visual inspection. If a belay device is dropped hard, and there is a question about its integrity, put it aside until thoroughly checked or discard it.
- Again, identify each piece of equipment with an etching pen, so that a usage log may be kept.

Helmets

Helmets are tough items. They have to be tough because of the job they may be called upon to do—fending off falling rocks and bumping against bolts, cables, or staples. Helmets need to be treated well so they will offer protection when needed.

- Do not drop or toss helmets. Helmets are not chairs to sit on while waiting. Avoid squeezing the helmet to see how far it will bend. It may crack.
- Some helmets come with a tag identifying its useful lifetime, look for it. If your helmets do not have such a tag, remember that plastic helmets have an approximate life of five years. Fiberglass helmets have a slightly longer lifetime.
- When using a helmet, check to see that the suspension system is attached on all points.
- If any rivets are popped, cracks appear, or chin strap buckles break, have the helmet evaluated by a qualified person to decide whether it can be fixed or not. New straps can be installed on helmets and can be purchased through a climbing shop or outdoor store.
- For hygiene purposes, regularly disinfect the inside of the helmet. Keep it clean and dry.

Notes

Figure 2-39.
Cracked helmet.

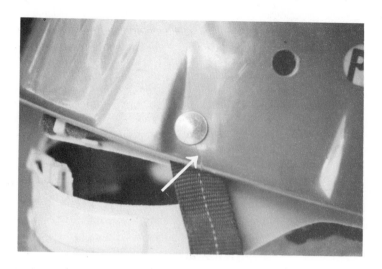

Rescue Blades, Rope Bag

- Keep the rope bag clean and free of debris, inside and out. Dry the bag prior to storing rope. Do not store wet rope in the bag.
- Keep knifes sharp or replace them as needed. Keep blades dry to prevent them from rusting.

Belay Gloves

- Buy gloves that fit *your* hands and that have leather on the palms and fingers. Rapidly moving nylon rope burns flesh—USE GLOVES.

NOTE: All equipment should be checked at regular intervals for signs of wear. Keep careful and consistent records on all equipment, and particularly the gear used for the Pamper Pole or rock climbing, noting times of use and numbers of falls. The average life for a polyester blend rope is two to three years. Kernmantle ropes are tested and recommended for a maximum of 2000 hours of use. Rope life depends on the variables of light, moisture, dirt, abrasion and hours of use.

Chapter 3

Rescues

"It is better to be prepared for an opportunity and not have one than to have an opportunity and not be prepared."   Whitney Young, Jr.

General Considerations

Whenever a group is working on the Ropes Course, the lead (ground) facilitator must have a harness at hand and know where the rescue kit is located in the event that an emergency requires an evacuation from the high course. Should such an emergency occur, the lead facilitator will be focused on one participant for several minutes. During this time, the other participants must be stabilized. If on a static course, all participants must go to the nearest platform or stationary point, remain clipped in, and not move again until given permission. **Each course should develop its own set of emergency procedures tailored to that course.**

In the vast majority of falls (slips) on a Ropes Course, the participant is unharmed and can simply climb back onto the element. If s/he is emotionally distraught, a facilitator can usually help verbally from the ground, or climb up, using a self-belay, and assist the participant in making a decision. A conscious participant should be able to hang safely in a commercial harness for at least 15 minutes. Having climbed to the participant, a helping hand and verbal instruction will usually relieve the situation. The use of a rope ladder is another means of helping the participant get repositioned on the element and continue.

Notes

Rescue Equipment

Figure 3-1.
Rescue bag.
Contents:
- Rescue Figure Eight
- Knife
- 3 Steel Locking Carabiners
- Static Rope
- Rope Ladder (Etrier)
- Prusik Cord

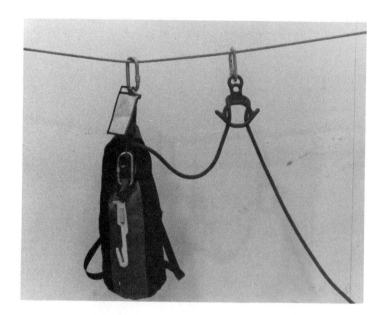

Rescue from Dynamic Belay

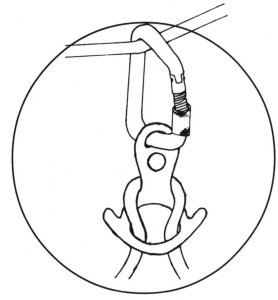

Figure A

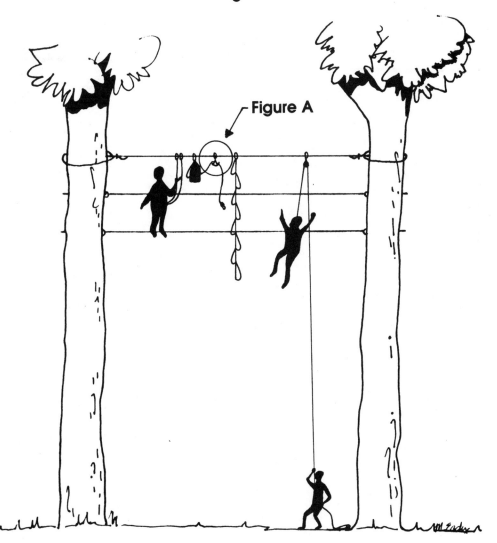

Figure 3-2a. Step 1. Rescue from dynamic belay.

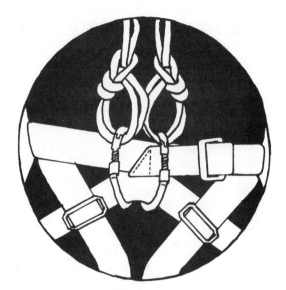

Figure B

Figure 3-2b. Step 2. Rescue from dynamic belay.

A dynamic rescue on a Ropes Course is extremely unlikely, particularly if a dynamic (sling shot) belay is being used. However, over the last 25 years I have seen a person get stuck half-way down a zip wire, a climber become tangled in a Hebbie Jeebie, and a participant on a high Ropes Course element become unable to continue, all of which required a rescue. If you need to perform a high Ropes Course rescue, here's a *basic* procedure that will get you and the climber down quickly and safely.

Scenario: A climber, on a dynamic belay, has fallen and becomes entangled in the element and cannot untangle him/herself.

Do this:

- Designate someone (and only that person) to communicate with the climber while you are preparing for the rescue.
- If a rescue kit is available, use it. If not, designate someone to obtain an 11 millimeter static rope long enough to extend from the event's belay cable to the ground and back. While the rope is being located, buckle on a commercial harness or tie on a Studebaker wrap. If the only rope you have available is a length of climbing rope, use it.
- Clip three steel locking carabiners into one another. Lock the gate of the center carabiner. Clip one of the end carabiners to the front of your harness; lock it. Leave the free end carabiner unlocked. If you can't find steel carabiners, use whatever you have on hand.
- Clip a set of lobster claws (bear claws, crab claws) into the front of your harness.
- Make sure you have a knife that is situated on the outside of your harness: i.e. not in a pocket. Use a rescue knife or surgical scissors if possible, but don't waste time looking for the perfect knife.
- Take a bight in one end of the rescue rope and reeve it through a Figure Eight descender as you would for rappelling. Tie a bowline on a bight, or whatever loop knot you can tie efficiently, into the working end of that rope. Use a locking carabiner to clip that loop to the front of your harness. Lock the carabiner.
- Connect a locking carabiner into the Figure Eight and clip it somewhere onto your harness (dominant side) so that you can procure it easily.
- Begin climbing one of the stapled trees that supports the element in question. Use lobster claws to protect yourself while climbing. If available, have someone act as a rope handler to facilitate your climb.
- When you get to the height of the belay cable, clip both of your claws to that cable.
- Unclip the Figure Eight from your harness, then clip it and the attached rescue rope to the belay cable. Lock and properly orient the carabiner. Attach the rescue rope bowline on a bight with a carabiner into your harness. Tell your belayer that you are "on belay" and wait for a "belay on" response. Once on belay, remove your claws from the belay cable.
- Move out onto the event until you are directly above or next to the dangling or entangled participant.
- Alert your belayer below that you are ready to be lowered to the victim. Tell the victim, in a confident voice, that you are coming to assist him/her.

Notes

- Orient yourself to the victim so that you are face to face. Clip the end carabiner of the three-in-line carabiners into the victim's carabiner (or directly into the harness if a Figure Eight Follow-Through tie-in knot had been used). Lock all carabiners.
- Untangle victim from element.
- Ask the victim, in a firm, steady voice, to grip your torso with their legs (scissors grip). Alert your belayer(s) that you are about to cut the climber's belay rope. Advise victim there will be a small jolt or drop when the rope is cut. With knife in hand, do a double check on which rope to cut, then orient the blade so the cutting motion is directed safely away from the victim. Close the blade (if it folds) and toss it *away* from the belayers or clip it to your harness if you can do so quickly and safely.
- After completing the cut, and while being lowered, grasp the victim with both arms in a bear hug. Say something comforting.
- The belayer(s) should be lowering you both to complete the rescue.

Rescue from Static Belay

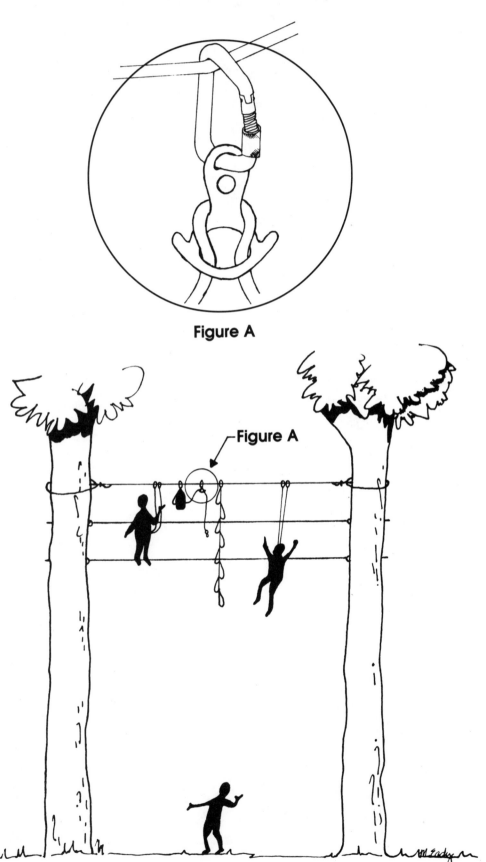

Figure A

Figure A

Figure 3-3a. Step 1. Rescue from static belay.

Figure B

Figure 3-3b. Step 2. Rescue from static belay.

All static courses should have rescue rope bags and a rope ladder up on the course, ready to use whenever the course is in operation. If participant is cooperating and coherent, slide the rope ladder out to her/him and ask s/he to put a foot into a loop and try to move back up and onto the element. Use of the rope ladder is sufficient in most situations. If this is not successful, connect the rope bag to the belay cable. From the rope bag, pull out the Rescue Figure 8 with attached steel carabiner and reeved rescue rope and properly attach and orient to the belay cable. Slide-walk, by use of lobster claws, out to the participant.

Ask participant to put his/her foot back into the loop of the rope ladder. The facilitator should attach the rope and carabiner, with the bowline-on-a-bight, to the participant's harness. After checking for clearance, drop the rope bag to the ground. The ground facilitator should assume a belay position. After going through the proper belay commands, the facilitator asks the participant to step up into the loop in order to take the weight off her/his lobster claws and disconnect the claws either from the harness or belay cable. If the participant cannot step up into the rope ladder and take the weight off their claws, then the facilitator must cut the participant free.

Note: Always check twice and then cut *away* from your claws and rescue rope.

After making sure the participant has cleared the element, s/he can be lowered safely to the ground. **Note:** ALWAYS insure that the ground belay system is securely in place before you disconnect the participant's lobster claws.

Note: Before using your Ropes Course, check the rescue rope bag for correct set up.

This material is designed to be used as a refresher, not as a primary means of rescue training information. All rescue training must be completed with and by a trained professional. Rescue skills are critical and should be kept fresh by constant practicing and training.

Chapter 4

Maintenance and General Inspection

by David Klim

General Considerations

It has been my experience that many owners or people in charge of Ropes Courses are not aware of the fact that their outdoor Ropes Courses will need upkeep. Like a house or car, small amounts of timely maintenance will stave off large expenditures later. A budget is needed to provide for scheduled maintenance. Outdoor Ropes Courses are ever-changing like a house and yard. House ownership demands occasional painting, replacement of a gutter or steps, some landscaping, and of course, always cutting the lawn. There is something to do continually even if it is not a big job. With outdoor Ropes Courses, trees grow, branches die or break in storms, poles shrink, the ground compacts under the feet of many participants, all of which need to be observed and taken care of so a course will remain safe, neat, and healthy! The effort is not that difficult, but it will require a person to be able to inspect every cable on a course. The majority of the maintenance to be done at heights may necessitate a ropes course builder/inspector. It is not recommended to work at a certain height if a person is not confident doing so.

What is recommended here are maintenance and upkeep tasks which all Ropes Course instructors should be able to accomplish. The items listed below will enable an instructor to identify potential maintenance and safety issues which will assure the safety of participants and longevity of the course.

Here is a general list of some tools that are good to have on hand to do basic maintenance on a Ropes Course: a ratchet handle and 3/4 inch socket, a ten inch curved jaw vice grips, a 10 inch or 12 inch adjustable wrench, a 2 1/2 pound hammer for staples, a claw hammer for nails, a branch cutter (loppers), a hand saw for branches or boards. These tools will get most jobs done. I'll save the winches, swagers, and chain saws for another time.

This chapter is divided into three sections. Each section looks at a specific part of a Ropes Course. Part I examines the environment. This includes the area around the course—the ground, the trees, animals, insects, and weather. Part II addresses wood items on a Ropes Course, such as walls and platforms. Part III focuses on inspections of metal items including all cable, nuts and bolts, etc.

Part I—Environmental

The environment is constantly changing. Just as dry, hot weather or wet and freezing weather takes its toll on a house, it has the same effect on a Ropes Course. When a Ropes Course is installed, changes begin to occur within that environment.

- If a Ropes Course is installed in an area which has not had heavy foot traffic, and has had areas cleared of bushes and saplings, the ground beneath the new activities will begin to pack down. These remaining punji-like sticks can trip up a spotter and become dangerous if fallen upon. They should be removed. Ground compaction is a threat to the health of the trees in the immediate area. Packing down the soil keeps water and oxygen from the roots. This can be prevented by spreading either wood chips or bark mulch where the most compaction has taken place, such as on the trail into the course and under each element. Wood chips are good, relatively cheap, and more readily available than bark mulch which is preferable although more costly. Tree companies may readily volunteer to donate chips. Ask them if the chips came from healthy or diseased trees. It matters to your trees since diseased chips will spread disease to your trees.

- Trees are susceptible to many problems. Diseases, weather, pollution, and insects are ever present to attack them. Keep an eye out for the health of your trees. Certain diseases and insects can damage or kill trees in a very short time. Ants can eat away the inside of a tree with hardly an outward sign. Caterpillars can eat the leaves and some beetles can bore through bark.

Figure 4-1. Insect infected tree. Notice saw dust at base.

- Remember, an element attached to a dead tree will not pass an inspection. If something looks very wrong about your trees, consult a tree surgeon or arborist. It may mean the saving of a tree on your course.

Figure 4-2. Element attached to deformed and weak tree.

- Bushes and overhanging branches reaching into an activity area need to be trimmed. This growth will happen quickly in a cleared forest area as the trees and bushes send out branches seeking sunlight.
- Watch for dead branches overhead which may present a danger. Have them removed. Do not wait for them to fall on their own; they might . . .
- After a windy day or a storm with rain or snow, check the course for broken and hanging branches anywhere in or near the course.

Figure 4-3. Fallen limbs near ropes course element.

Notes

- Dead trees in the vicinity or trees which have fallen need to be taken down completely.
- Animals may sometimes "set up house" at your Ropes Course. Burrowing animals may undermine trees. Squirrels may make nests in tires on the course or in trees. Squirrel holes in high element trees indicate the tree is hollow. If any high element's cable is above a squirrel hole then the element has a very good chance of failing the next inspection. There is more leeway on low activities built into trees with defects.
- Lightning damage can render a tree unusable. If a tree shows telltale signs of a lightning strike, i.e. bark blown off in a long thin strip(s) possibly in a spiral fashion down the length of the tree, there is no telling how much damage has been done. The wood could have been cracked through the trunk thus opening it up for insect invasion. The Ropes Course cables in one tree could have conducted the current to another tree creating more damage. Ropes Course cables and connections are not designed to conduct electricity to the ground. If a strike has happened on a course, a professional arborist and Ropes Course inspector need to be called in to assess tree health and course integrity.

Figure 4-4. Rotten cavity due to lightning strike.

- Insects like bees and ants can create a serious health situation with their bites and stings. On courses which are not used often, bees, wasps, yellow jackets, etc. can make nests on the undersides of swinging tires, walls and platforms, trees, and in the ground. Check these areas prior to use and take proper precautions. Be aware of ant hills hidden in tall grass, under mulched areas, and forest duff. Shift your location for sit-down games or posterior-oriented debriefs away from them.

Part II—Wood Items and Telephone Poles

On many Ropes Courses there are elements which are at least partly made from wood. These include walls, platforms, trolleys, and poles. The wood used is almost always pressure treated and will last far longer outside than untreated wood. When planning on using these activities, look at the general condition of the items and ask yourself some questions regarding them.

- Is the item solid upon shaking? It should be. If not, check to see if it can be tightened or made more secure? Check to see if the boards are still in good shape or need replacing. Kick at Hickory Jump stumps or Jus-rite descender poles to see if they are loose. If they are, pack down the dirt tightly around them or drive in a pressure treated shim.
- Has weathering caused severe cracking? Are the cracks on the wall wide enough to get fingers caught in? If this is a problem, fill the cracks with silicone caulking to keep fingers out.

Figure 4-5. Crack in wall due to lumber shrinkage.

- What about splinters or any sharp edges that could be rounded off? Remove the splinters and smooth the area. With sharp edges, quickly shave with a plane, or better yet a Sur Form file (looks like a cheese grater).

Figure 4-6. Sur Form tool.

- Are there any nail heads sticking up? If so, pound them down.
- Does a board seem rotten or loose? Pull out the rotted boards and replace them. With loose boards, reattach and or tighten them in the same way they were installed, unless the way has proven to be unreliable.

Notes

Figure 4-7. Exposed nails due to lumber shrinkage.

- Any bees underneath? Hope not! Use your preferred way to safely remove them if they have made a home on your course. Remember that a single sting on a person who is allergic to bees can turn a fun activity into a deadly situation.
- One problem which happens to platform braces built on trees is that as the tree grows in diameter it pushes the boards out with it; the lag screws (which are most commonly used to secure the braces to the tree) stay put. The result is that the board is forced over the lag screws and washers. This movement slowly destroys the board. When an indent is noticeable around a lag screw and washer on a board screwed to a tree, take your socket wrench and carefully turn the lag screw counter clockwise one-half to one full turn. This loosens or backs out the screw. The washer should not be loose when you are finished. Due to tree growth, check all lag screws yearly.

Figure 4-8. Board being forced past bolts and washers due to tree diameter growth.

- When there are items which are not made of pressure treated wood such as a log used for a Cat Walk, TP Shuffle, Hickory Jump stumps, Pamper Pole or Vertical Pole and Tire, these need a little special attention. Once or twice a year a quick application of wood preservative on these items will increase their longevity and delay expensive replacements. Check the integrity of these items by sticking a screwdriver into a part which looks the most rotten. If the screwdriver sinks in less than a half of an inch and the log beyond that point is so solid that the screwdriver will not go in any further with force, then the log is probably fine and just needs a coat of preservative. Conduct this test at a few points along a log TP Shuffle or Cat Walk. To check a log buried in the ground, realize that most of the decay will be at two points. One is on the top, the other is just below the surface of the ground. On top is an area where water, ice and snow collect and rot wood. Put plenty of preservative on the ends; these ends tend to drink up any liquid so one might as well let them drink up preservative. The transition zone is where the wood meets the ground plus a few inches. Scrape away some earth from around the stump or log about five inches down. Take the screwdriver and stick it into the log in the now exposed area to check how much has rotted. If the screwdriver pries out inches of rotted, punky wood, then it is time to replace this stump or log.

- Taking care of some of these wood problems using a little maintenance with tools or wood preservative can hold off large replacement costs for years. Do it now; do not become a victim of ropes course sticker shock.
- **Remember if you are not confident with the integrity of anything on a Ropes Course, it is best NOT to use an element while waiting for a professional opinion.**

Poles are not immune to damage from animals, age, and the weather.

- On occasion a pole or series of pole stumps in a line of Hickory Jump stumps can exhibit some rot in the ends. This usually is in the form of hollowing out the core creating a cup or bowl shape. Depending on how advanced the damage is, it may be taken care of with preservative and some filler or it may be that the log end needs to be trimmed back or totally replaced.
- A pole on a Ropes Course can, in a rare instance, develop a longitudinal crack. This often happens as a result of a new pole with a flaw in it from drying out quickly.
- In unusual instances, animals can damage poles. If holes appear in poles as a result of a neurotic woodpecker (it happens) ask a ropes course inspector for an evaluation. Big holes weaken the pole.

Figure 4-9. Woodpecker holes.

Figure 4-10. Woodpecker holes.

Notes

- Ropes Courses constructed with poles have a special consideration which is not true if trees are used. When a course is constructed with new poles the poles will shrink slightly over time allowing the nuts to become loose on the bolts. After six months or a year each nut will need to be tightened. This can be done by a facilitator earlier as needed but it should be done as part of the first year's safety inspection by a professional Ropes Course inspector.

Big Trouble

Part III—Metal Items

Items made of metal on a Ropes Course can be categorized as either cable or anything else other than cable, i.e. bolts, cable clamps, serving sleeves, etc.

- Some maintenance on a Ropes Course can be done by a facilitator, for example, tightening nuts on bolts or clamps. Other maintenance regarding replacing bolts and cable should be left to a professional.
- **Do NOT attempt any maintenance you are not comfortable and competent doing.**
- A reminder for people in charge of a Ropes Course is to have a budget in place for a yearly inspection, repairs, new elements, tree and grounds care, staffing, etc. The cost of building a course is not the end of the expenditures.
- Cable, or wire rope, should always be galvanized. The cable should be a 7 x 19 all steel construction. Simply described this means that the cable has seven separate bundles each containing 19 strands of wire. The 19 strands of wire are wound around each other creating a bundle. Seven bundles wound around each other form the cable. When looking at the cable from the outside, only six bundles are seen. The seventh is in the center and can be seen by looking at the end. The bundle in the middle is made of steel. Other styles of cable have a core bundle made of rope often known as plow cable. This type of inexpensive rope core has lower strength and holds rain water inside the core of the rope which promotes rusting from the inside out.
- In time, cable does rust even if it is galvanized. Different climates and quality of galvanization determine how quickly rust begins. Rust that can be scratched off with a fingernail is only on the surface and is okay. Rust causing pits in the strands, broken strands, or even severe discoloration is not okay and should be examined by a ropes course builder/inspector. If a cable looks slightly rusty, it does not necessarily mean that it needs to be replaced. If rust looks heavy, replacement will probably be needed. Look at the cable where it bends around the bolt. This is where strands that have been rusted through will most likely be found. If any strands are rusted through, then the cable should be replaced. Cable replacement is a job for a ropes course builder. Proper cable heights, tension, attachments and tools are needed for a job which is best left to a person with experience, not to the person who wants to experiment. Note that cables on low elements which support many people at the same time undergo more stress than most high element belay cables. Be assured that cables are strong and that new cables are extremely hard to break and generally hold up even when trees fall across them.
- Check the ends of the cable for fraying. Cable on any activity which has its end frayed is a hazard even if it is up high. The wires act like needles and can easily penetrate skin even after going through the side of a sneaker or glove. Frayed cable ends can temporarily be held down with tape. Preferably a serving sleeve should be used. These are small curled pieces of metal which are crimped around the end of the cable holding it to the main cable. They are almost permanent, they look professional, and they are cheap and easy to install.

Notes

Figure 4-11. Loose serving sleeve.

- Cables should always be smooth to the touch, especially cables where there is hand contact. If there are any sharp or broken strands or filings present, consult a professional Ropes Course vendor as to what should be done and what caused the damage.

Figure 4-12. Frayed cable end.

- Metal on Ropes Courses should always be plated with something to make it impervious to rust (supposedly). Metal sometimes does rust even if it is galvanized, but hot dipped galvanization is the norm for bolts and other hardware on a course and generally resists rust very well.
- Cable clamps, along with cable, generally show rust first.
- As an instructor on a Ropes Course, a quick look at the hardware can decide whether a closer inspection is needed. Showing up at an old course for the first time can be full of unhappy surprises. Rust as well as other problems mentioned here may be rampant.
- Aside from rust-related problems, tree growth can become a problem over time. As the tree grows it can envelop the ends of the bolts and cables.

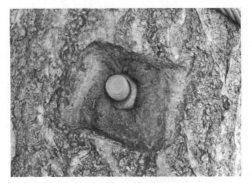

Figure 4-13. Tree growth over nut end of bolt.

- All of the cable needs to be visible. If a tree has grown to the degree that new growth covers cable, a new bolt should be installed leaving the old bolt in place. This growth process takes years to achieve and is not a surprise unless you are seeing the course for the first time.

Figure 4-14. Cable is girdling tree.   **Figure 4-15.** Overgrown thimble eye-bolt.

- Be aware of the tightness of all the nuts on the bolts and cable clamps. Keep them very tight.
- Replace any missing nuts.
- The pull on the bolt on all new ropes courses is in a straight line with the cable. There are older courses which had activities constructed with cables pulling 90 degrees to the bolts. This tended to bend the bolts and hurt the trees and is not an accepted method today. If this is the case on your course, have it adjusted to comply with A.C.C.T. standards.
- Staples need to be installed deeply so as to be solid, with no movement when weight is applied. A staple hammered in 3 inches will achieve this. Growth will eventually cover staples making them hard to climb on. Install new staples when this happens.

Figure 4-16. Vandalized strand vice.

Chapter 5

Knots

Knot Tips

If you had a bad experience trying to learn knots in the Boy Scouts or had trouble moving from page to reality in a knot book, here's a suggestion. Get together with someone who *likes* rope and knots and is willing to show you, vis-a-vis, what they look like, how they work, when to use a particular bend, what rope to use, how ropes differ in texture, and eventually how to feel good about using the right rope and knot in context of what you need at the moment. And, the "moment" is obviously not static; as the tension, pull, or strain changes so does the situational knot.

Knots aren't just knots. All the bends, tucks, splices and hitches are part of a bigger learning package that can be as simple or as complex as you want it to be. Knots represent craft, an avocation, a means of spending pleasant time, an image and the absolutely best way to temporarily attach one thing to another.

But we are here—in the book—and you need to know a few knots. (Don't forget what I suggested above, find a friendly person who likes knots. . . .)

Specific knot tips:

- Get a section of supple rope that's easy on the hands. Practicing with an old piece of tarred manila hemp isn't the greatest.
- Purchase a current knot tying book that photographically and pictorially displays the tying sequences so clearly that you *want* to give the knot a try. May we suggest *Forget Me Knots*, written by Karl Rohnke and published by Kendall/Hunt.
- Learning a knot involves the process of doing the same thing over and over again, eventually imprinting those cranial motor pathways in such a way that the knot sequence becomes automatic. This takes time. If you tie a knot just a couple of times, try to recall the sequence a couple days later; gone . . . goodbye.

Knot Illustrations

Here's a minimal list of knots for use on a Ropes Course. You can always learn more, but knowing these (I mean KNOWING) will get you through just about any high Ropes Course situation.

Check out Plynn Williams' artistic flair in clearly depicting not only the knot but how to tie it. Plynn and I collaborated on a knot book (*Forget Me Knots*, referenced earlier) a few years ago that covers only knots specific to a Ropes Course.

Bowline-on-a-Bight—is the knot that many programs use in the end of their belay line. Then it is connected to a climber's harness with a locking carabiner.

Figure 5-1.
Bowline-on-a-Bight/
Safety Knot.

Benefits of this knot include: a high test breaking strength, two finished loops to clip into, and an ease in untying. I have towed pick-up trucks with rope connected to the vehicle using a bowline-on-a-bight, and then easily untied the knot at the destination.

There's only one drawback that I can think of; unless this knot is backed up with a safety knot, it can loosen itself. If tension is consistently applied on the knot, there is generally no problem with loosening.

Overhand Knot—is probably the simplest of knots, and learned in this context primarily doubled (x two) for use as a safety knot. This doubled safety knot (tunnel, barrel, or half a fisherman's knot) is used to protect every primary knot on a ropes course.

Figure 5-2. Overhand Knot.

Square Knot—is basically, two overhand knots tied on top of one another. This knot by itself is unreliable, but it is used extensively on Ropes Courses as the finishing knot for the *Studebaker wrap*. The reason for this apparent safety paradox is that the knot is never used alone. Double safety (tunnel, barrel, half fisherman) knots are *always* used on either side of the square knot.

Consider—most of the students that climb on a ropes course will probably never take up climbing as a sport. The emphasis is not to teach them a fancy technical system for tying in, but to show them something that they can learn quickly and apply to their own efforts of tying on a harness. The argument that the *Studebaker wrap* takes too long to tie begs these questions: What's the rush? What are you trying to achieve by using a commercial harness? Are you trying to get the students ready faster? Are you trying to see how many elements they can get through? Isn't tying on a wrap part of the responsibility for self that is being emphasized?

Granny Knot (not illustrated)—is a square knot tied unsymmetrically. It is more unreliable than the square knot. Take the time to retie it.

Figure Eight Loop—is very easy to tie and identify (it looks like an "8"). It provides a convenient, no slip, clip-in loop for climbing. It's only drawback is that the knot has a tendency to jam under tension. But, by providing one more twist to the tying sequence results in a "Figure Nine" (does not look like a "9," but offers a knot that is less likely to jam). Use a Figure Eight or nine loop only if you forget how to tie a bowline-on-a-bight, or how to fashion a figure eight follow through. It's funny that, ". . . if you forget how to tie a bowline-on-a-bight, tie lots of whatever you do remember," this is true and may save some skin.

Figure 5-3.
Figure Eight Loop.

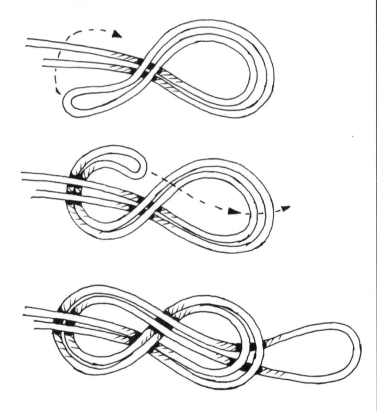

Figure Eight Follow-Through—is another Figure Eight variation that is used extensively by climbers. Tying-in using this knot sequence precludes the use of a carabiner, which gets rid of an unnecessary link in the belay chain.

Studebaker Wrap—is a self-tied custom fitted pelvic harness that can be clipped into front or back. (Commercial harness makers generally do not guarantee their harnesses for a rear clip-in.) This well tried and tested self-tied harness is much less expensive and usually better fitting than a commercial harness made of webbing. The commercial harness, however, allows a higher level of comfort than is available from any tied harness.

Figure 5-4.
Studebaker Wrap.

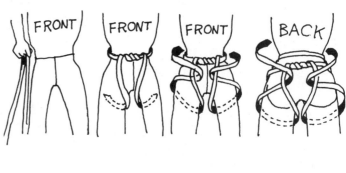

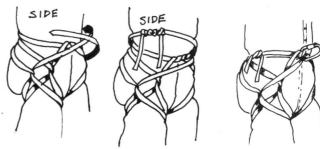

Prusik Knot—knowing this esoteric knot and how to apply it is an undeniable image maker, and it's not that difficult to tie. Its application varies from tying a Lobster Claw self belay system to its use in ascending gymnasium climbing ropes. More mundane functions include securing a tent fly or tying down a rack-top load on a vehicle.

Figure 5-5. Prusik Knot.

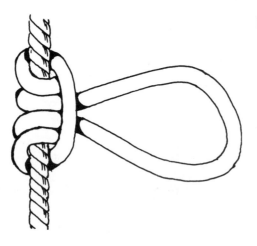

Killick Hitch—the Killick Hitch is made up of a Clove Hitch and Half Hitch tied in sequence. The function of this combination of hitches is to allow a means of pulling a climbing rope up and through a shear reduction device using a 1/8 inch diameter section of nylon cord as the hauling line. The nylon cord is tied onto the working end of a climbing rope by using the Killick Hitch.

Figure 5-6. Killick Hitch.

Water Knot—if you need a secure knot to join two ends of webbing, the Water Knot is your best choice. Check it out, because the illustration shows much more than I can pass along with words. Leave enough tail so that each end of webbing can be entirely grabbed by your hand (approximately 3 1/2 inches).

Figure 5-7.
Water Knot.

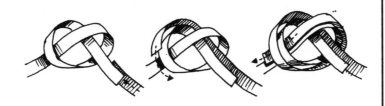

Taking Participants Through the Course

Preparation and Staffing

Preparation of Client Group

Initial Contact and Contract

Be honest and straight forward about what services you can and cannot provide. Be firm and consistent with your standards.

Negotiate:
- Time allowed to complete experience
- Standard of participation
- Goals of the group (this will determine which events you choose to utilize, in order to provide the best experience)
- Schedule payment and rain date

Other Data

Adult Leaders' Roles—In general, if adults participate, children tend to expect them to take leadership roles. This limits self-discovery. Find a way to include the adults as assistants to the facilitator/staff, run youth/adults separately, or get a commitment from adults to assume a lesser role.

Group Size—Get a commitment as to the group size. Groups of six are too small for good group dynamics and groups of 24 are too cumbersome. However, with a proper size course and staff you could serve a larger group by dividing them into subgroups of 15–20.

Background—Collect information about your upcoming program, such as type of group, age range, composition of group, and previous experiences together. Some of this information will come from the preparation meeting, and it is important because it will help you determine the following:

- Whether to focus on individual events or group problem-solving activities.
- How much time to spend on the different aspects of the course.

Notes

Logistics
- Set dates for the preparation meeting, Ropes Course, and follow-up.

The Pre-Meeting*

The pre-meeting is an integral part of a Ropes Course experience. All staff and participants should attend.

This meeting gives you a chance to assess the group, determine the goals and standards for the day, and to enlighten the group about what to expect. It is also an opportunity for the client group to get to know the staff and to become more familiar with your standards and expectations.

Plan some creative way to introduce the Ropes Course. A slide program or photo album can be an effective way to present your course. Be careful, however, to avoid overwhelming participants with too many visuals. Playing a game or asking a series of reflective questions works as well in setting the stage.

Elicit individual and group goals from group. You may wish to have the entire staff participate. Recording goals on a flipchart or blackboard helps emphasize their importance. As a facilitator, you will want to remember the original goals and be able to refer back to them throughout the Ropes Course.

Distribute handouts and necessary participation forms. Get clear verbal commitment that participants understand and agree to abide by the agreed upon goals and standards. These forms include clothing list, informed consent, medical information and authorization, and assumption of risk/voluntary release.

Be firm. Setting a firm, safety-conscious tone here will avoid problems later. Make it clear that breaching rules is unacceptable. Your format may vary for youth and adults.

Make arrangements for bad weather. Develop alternate plans and be sure to get contacts and phone numbers.
*See Appendix II for Sample Pre-Meeting Schedule

Staff Preparation

The Ropes Course event is an intense, compressed experience. It cannot be stressed strongly enough that staff benefit from adequate preparation time, as well as time to "cool out" and debrief.

The staff should meet to discuss the event beforehand—regardless of whether they have worked together in the past. One hour is generally adequate. This provides time to discuss the previous preparation meeting, work out a plan to satisfy the goals of the group, make staff assignments, and review medical forms if available. It is also time to work out strategies for inclement weather as well as various options for working with the group (for example: if seven people show up instead of ten, it may require altering your plans, or you may consider calling the experience off). See Chapter 1 for staff ratios. Decide who will take equipment to the course and who will set up each event. Ensure that each facilitator has a copy of the schedule that includes staff assignments.

Day of the Event

One Hour Before the Group Arrives

Meet to set up the course and give the staff a little time to relax before the group comes. This will also give you time to review medical forms and work out any final details.

When the Group Arrives

Collect any due forms and money before you get started. Seat the group, review goals, standards, and facilitators roles, and get a recommitment from the group. You are not a participant; don't try to be one. You are there to facilitate personal growth and development. You are a model, and your behavior and methods of dealing with others will set the tone for the group.

At the Beginning of the Program

Get acquainted by using a name game, such as Name Echo. Next, address goals and standards.

Minimum Goals:
- Have safe fun!
- Work on communicating with, and taking care of one another.
- Challenge yourself. Do something difficult, stretch your boundaries.
- Respect others.

Minimum Standards:
- Must have required signed forms, in order to participate.
- Try!
- No alcohol or non-prescription drugs.
- Stay with the group. Keep off elements unless under staff supervision.

Minimum Housekeeping:
- Location of bathroom.
- Remember your belongings. Take out whatever you bring in.
- Walk only on trails; do not stray off them.
- Do not alter the landscape.
- Be careful when walking. Watch out for potholes and eye-level sticks.
- Empty pockets and remove jewelry so as not to injure yourself and others.
- Determine tobacco policy.

Facilitator/Adult Roles: Facilitator's role is to give instructions, watch for safety, and to facilitate the group's discussion. Other adult roles should be negotiated.

Medical Issues: Ask the group about medical issues. Allow participants to disclose any recent injuries, bad backs, problem knees, etc. This disclosure serves the dual purpose of reinforcing the concept of personal limitations as well as soliciting help in taking care of oneself and others. If the

Notes

participant becomes uncomfortable, it is his/her responsibility to let the group know.

Confirm the Group's Commitment Agreement: With some groups this is a time to state firmly that if they don't abide by the contract or if they are not participating safely, they will be required to go home (varies for youth and adults).

Activities Presented During the Day

Presentation:
1. Facilitator explains the challenge and objectives.
2. Facilitator demonstrates, when appropriate.
3. Facilitator gets a clear commitment to do the activity.
4. Group does the activity.
5. Group reflects on and begins to discuss the activity.
6. Facilitator utilizes the Experiential Learning Cycle (or other method) to process the activity.

Be Flexible Personally and with the Time Schedule. Listen to and rely on your intuition. A schedule is only a tool from which to work. YOU HAVE PERMISSION TO THROW IT OUT! In some cases you can make this decision, in others, you may ask the participants to do so, based upon choices that you provide. Do your best to coordinate these changes with other staff.

Evaluation—Close Out

An in-depth listing of facilitation and reflection questions is covered elsewhere in this manual. A review of this material will assist in developing your own format for final evaluations.

Group on the Group
1. Did they enjoy it? Why? Why not?
2. Individual insights on group interaction, cohesion, areas for improvement.
3. "What I learned about my group," with appropriate feedback to one another.
4. A final affirmation, ending on a positive note.

Staff on Group—Based on Goals
1. Review of group and individual goals.
2. Were they accomplished? How? What prevented them?
3. What constructive learnings can be applied to everyday life?

Group on Staff
1. Group comments on staff: personal reflections as well as overall event.
2. Did participants feel comfortable, supported and challenged?
3. Did the group feel safe regarding facilitators technical skills?

After the Program, Staff Processing

Debrief, share experiences and critique roles of each facilitator. This should be an open forum where sharing is encouraged, interruptions are minimal, and mutual respect is mandatory. It may be pleasant to share this time over a beverage or a meal.

Evaluation of Staff by Staff. It is best for this to be an ongoing process that starts when you first come together as a team. For example, you may begin by looking at the central issues of teamwork. This review can be as structured or informal as you wish. A basic list of questions follows. You may think of others that are applicable to your particular staff.

- What kind of support would I like to have?
- What kind of support do I require of you? Have I clearly identified and communicated this to you?
- What technical skills of mine (a) are good, (b) could use refinement?
- Do we tend to be more task-oriented or more focused on group process? Are we able to balance these two roles?
- What is my style of leadership and facilitation?
- What is my style of conflict management with staff and participants?
- What are my values in facilitating a course? Seek to reach balance for polarized values. (This will help you to identify how styles differ and how one may complement another).
- How do we accomplish our goals and objectives when we work with groups?
- How can we continually improve our performance?
- Do we practice shared leadership?
- What can we do to improve our process?

Follow-up

It is important to hold a follow-up meeting whenever possible. This is most effective when held within two to three weeks of the program. Participants will have integrated what was learned, and yet the experience and enthusiastic memories will be fresh in their minds. Written feedback is an excellent method through which participants may express insights that do not surface during the discussion.

Staff Preparation Check List

For Operating a Ropes Course, Games, Initiatives, or Any Type of
Outdoor Adventure Program

Prior to Program

*This list will help facilitators check for adequate preparation for an
upcoming program.*

• Become familiar with the group's goals, objectives, and composition
(age, gender, reason for participation, etc.).

• Review all medical forms. Note special cases so that you may observe
caution in appropriate situations.

• Check weather report, prepare for forecasted weather and arrange
back-up plans.

• Inspect all gear for wear and condition. Provide necessary maintenance to the gear.

• Inventory First Aid Kit contents and restock if necessary.

• Walk the course and check its overall condition. Remove all hazards,
such as downed branches, and visually inspect all elements. This is in
addition to regular inspections for maintenance.

• Meet with all facilitators. Ensure that everyone is familiar with their
roles and the overall "game plan."

• Review emergency procedures. Ensure emergency phone numbers
and maps to emergency facilities are clearly posted.

High Course Operations Check List

Prior to, and During a Program

Attending to these details, before and after the participants arrive, will foster the safe operations of a high course.

Emergency Systems
- Each staff member must know the Emergency Plan and evacuation or rescue procedures for this particular course.
- Have easy access to all medical forms.
- On courses where rescue bags are used, check each one prior to each program for proper packing and condition.
- All facilitators should have immediate access to, or carry, a closed knife or emergency scissors, extra carabiners, and two prusik or sewn runners.
- Each facilitator should have the knowledge, ability, and confidence to rappel off a high course element using proper safety gear.
- Keep an eye out for weather conditions. Know the quickest exit system in case of sound of approaching thunder or a sign of lightning.

Facilitator Positions
- Always operate a static course with at least one facilitator on the ground to ensure proper hook-up and the sending of participants into the course, as well as a back-up for emergency situations.
- *No participant* should enter a static course until there is a facilitator up on the course.
- Always operate a dynamic course with at least one facilitator on the ground, who is *not* belaying, and can serve as a back-up for emergency situations.

Participants
- Be sure participants have been **double checked** for proper fit and assembly of equipment (harness, buckles, belay apparatus) before beginning course. **This cannot be stressed enough!!!** Establish a checking system among your staff that is adhered to in every situation.
- Make sure that each participant has been properly instructed and has demonstrated the proper use of safety equipment. *Require absolute attention during demonstration times. When preparing to demonstrate, wait until you have everyone's full attention. Make it very clear to the participants that their safety is dependent upon careful and correct usage of their equipment.*
- All participants should participate in activities of their own free will. Excessive physical, mental, or emotional prompting or coercion is strongly discouraged. **Note:** if you intimidate someone into doing something that they "don't want to do" it could become an issue in a liability case.
- Check each person as he/she moves through the course for his/her physical, mental, and emotional state. Review the group periodically to keep a situational pulse on everyone. Take measures necessary to provide non-invasive support.

Notes

Low Course Operations Check List

Prior to, and During a Program

Attending to these details, before and after the participants arrive, will foster the safe operation of a low course.

Keep a Pulse on All Systems
- Each facilitator must know where first aid kits are located, as well as emergency procedures for your particular course.
- Each facilitator must have easy access to all medical forms.
- Visually inspect each event as you arrive at the site. This will be just a double-check, since it should have been accomplished before the program began.
- Keep a check on the weather. Consider what steps to take should conditions become threatening (i.e. rain gear or moving indoors).
- **Always** have water available. Plan adequate time for water, bathroom breaks, and meals.
- Be sure that participants have proper clothing and footwear. Remove all jewelry and watches. Get rid of gum, candy, or chewing tobacco which could be swallowed during activities.
- Continually monitor group for attention level, energy level, hypothermia, dehydration, and heat exhaustion. Have a plan to remedy negative situations as they occur.
- Get into the habit of scanning the area and making eye contact (to check in) with other facilitators every few minutes. This "check in" ensures that you can catch another facilitator's attention non-verbally when required.

Communication
- Maintain a firm and compassionate safety-conscious tone.
- On low elements which require a demonstrated technique in order to ensure safety, be sure that *all* safety aspects have been covered before commencing. Be aware that if you always demonstrate an event, you negate the participants' potential performance.
- Always be sure that a communication process is in effect before participants begin events which require spotting (example: "Spotters ready?" reply: "Ready!").
- Don't hesitate to stop an event to regain control or to avert a potential accident.
- Consistently give clear verbal commands. Ask questions. Find out participants' needs and take time to create "space" for them to speak out. *Practice two-way communication, talking and listening.*
- Silently observe the group, keep track of the physical, mental, and emotional state of participants. Make adjustments to provide support when needed without distracting or detracting from the activities of the entire group.
- Encourage participants to identify and share their hopes for the experience. Give them enough time to process the request and formulate a response.
- Discuss what group goals they are hoping to accomplish.
- Facilitators may offer appropriate goals at this time.

Opening and Closing
of an Outdoor Event with a Client Group

It is as important to open smoothly, clearly, and harmoniously as it is to close with a summation of learning, and a positive affirmation for the participants and their work.

A disorganized opening sets a tone of confusion for clients and staff. A closing that is hurried, with insufficient time to process, diminishes the day's accomplishments.

Be sure to schedule adequate time for opening and closing. Remember to share leadership with the entire staff, dividing responsibility for these opening and closing sessions.

Opening

- **Begin by forming a circle.** Wait for everyone. Let everyone know that you will not begin until everyone is there. Peer pressure will alert the tardy.
- State, **"Welcome to the Ropes Course"** or something else appropriate to the event and the group. Observe each person silently and try to assimilate their attitudes.
- **Play a name game.** Choose a game that helps set the stage for a comfortable, non-threatening day.
- **Have each person identify and share what they are hoping to accomplish.** Proceed slowly, easily, and deliberately.
- **Let participants know what the facilitators' roles will be.** Look at each person as you communicate in order to be sure that he/she clearly understands.
- **Communicate housekeeping guidelines.** Again, look at each person to assess comprehension.
- **Review the standards, one at a time and slowly. Check for each participant's agreement.** See *Preparation and Staffing section for complete checklist.*

  - No alcohol or other non-prescription drugs.
  - Give everything a try. "Failing forward" is definitely a part of learning.
  - Look out for yourself as well as others. Ask for help and support when you need it. If you experience pain or discomfort, let a facilitator know. Injury can become worse by continuing. We will make arrangements for you to participate in ways that will not aggravate the injury and administer first aid when necessary. It is very important to state this because often participants may not speak up should an injury occur.

- **Briefly discuss the day's schedule.** Include major divisions of the day such as lunch and closing time. A more specific break-down of the schedule is unnecessary. Check with everyone for agreement. Find out if anyone has to leave early so that you can plan for it.
- **Take final questions** and then begin the warm-ups.

- **Warm-ups.** This is the final section of the opening. Facilitators participate in the warm-ups in order to demonstrate *inclusion*. Once finished, facilitators return to a supportive background role, and the group solves initiative games on their own.

Sample Sequence with Demonstration by Facilitator
- Stretching exercises
- Illustrate Spotting, demonstrating which areas of body to protect
- Demonstrate and practice lifting (safely)
- Tag games
- **Complete the Opening.** Go on to first **initiative game**.

Emphasize moving carefully and deliberately, and keep the participants with you each step of the way. Repeat a clear statement of personal commitment to let all parties know what is expected. To keep the tempo from dragging, make your explanations brief and to the point. *Be supportive and enthusiastic.*

Closing

Closing takes place after the final group initiative of the day. This does not replace a planned, structured, follow-up meeting after the program.

- **SOLO.** Why solo? This allows time to reflect on what the day has meant to participants. After the last initiative, you may choose to send the participants out to find a quiet, private spot for five to fifteen minutes. Initiate recall with a loud noisemaker.
- **Return and form a circle.**
- **What specific feedback do you have for anyone about today's activities?** You may solicit one positive or helpful comment from each person.
- **Ask for comments on what they experienced and/or learned, either as individuals or as a group.** Provide an opportunity to focus on thoughts and feelings.
- **Ask for final feedback for the facilitators.** Inquire about safety, comfort level, and ask what helpful things the facilitators did. This is an excellent opportunity to ask for specific suggestions for improvements.
- **Express thanks from the entire staff and compliment them genuinely.** Close on a positive note and express your hope that they return to the Ropes Course. Remember to make arrangements for the follow-up meeting or the next day's program, whichever is applicable.

Chapter 7

Facilitation

Ropes Course Model

The Ropes Course is made up of a series of trust-building activities, individual events, and group problem-solving events, also known as initiatives. Each activity or event requires the group to work as a team in order to achieve results based upon concrete and preplanned objectives. Staff members are facilitators and do not participate in team activities, their goal is to assist the group in becoming a cohesive and effective team. (Facilitators may participate in ice-breakers, warm-ups, or spot or lift when necessary.)

The style and attitude of the facilitators have a great influence on how participants perceive the experience. A playful and lighthearted demeanor goes a long way towards making the Ropes Course appear as an adventure, rather than a threat. For the average person, ropes course events are a new and unusual way to learn self confidence and esteem. Therefore, it is essential that every effort should be made to keep the participants relaxed, comfortable, and involved, while maintaining an atmosphere that is pleasant and enjoyable. Safety is always a serious consideration, and should be foremost in the mind of a facilitator, while at the same time, the experienced facilitator manages easily to flow with the needs of the participants.

The Team Concept

The *team* is the central focus of any Ropes Course event. Its development is a goal that attention should be focused on repeatedly. The most effective way in which to do this is to take all conflicts, criticisms, and decisions directly to the team, and assist them in working out these challenges. Don't suppress conflict. Stop the activity and begin reflecting and processing immediately. This will resolve the conflict when appropriate, while it is still fresh in the minds of everyone. Avoid imposing your decisions and issues on the group.

Facilitator Role—The Quiet Authority

You (the facilitator) are in charge! The first hour of activity should make this very clear. The experience is designed with the intent of having the group develop into a team over time. Therefore, the team should gradually

Notes

become more autonomous and capable of problem-solving among themselves. You may have to exercise some control and supervision depending on the type of group and type of activity. Work on passing control to the members; taking conflict and criticism directly to the team helps place control in the members hands.

Once the team recognizes that you'll consistently wait for them to deal with matters, conflict begins to take care of itself. Your job is to facilitate growth, not to intimidate, prod, or hassle. Each person has agreed to try everything. Stretching and/or challenging must be left as a decision of the participant, particularly in regards to individual challenges. Help the group by providing support to those who are afraid of some events. Don't get *too* involved in either supporting or prodding. Peer pressure will often take care of this. Affirm the individual's self-worth, and then let the team play the supportive role. If you don't disengage at some level, you may become a subtle member of the team and may lose authority to facilitate effectively. The team deserves to experience success on its own, without being confused by your involvement as part of the process.

Your significant role is to ensure that participants have the opportunity to reflect on individual and group challenges. Often, reflection periods are short, especially with youth, who have difficulty expressing themselves verbally. Still, this time is very important because individuals need to know that their feelings and ideas are valued and respected.

Active Listening

Effective listening is at the core of all meaningful processing. Active listening includes understanding what the speaker is saying and is also a process by which the listener identifies, accepts, and verbalizes (reflects) the feelings that the speaker is experiencing.

Active listening is a very important skill that requires patience, the ability to be empathetic, and a lot of practice. Listening for feelings is often at the heart of inter- and intrapersonal problems and communications. Without an active effort to bring out feelings into the open, they often remain hidden. Remember, many people are not aware of their own feelings or are unable to define the source of their general discomfort. Further in this chapter, you will find a list of questions that help bring out feelings into the open.

Processing

"If you give a man a fish, he will have a single meal; if you teach him how to fish, he will eat all his life." Kuan-Tzu

If facilitators would practice the many skills involved in successful processing with the same diligence that they practice first aid skills and knot tying, Ropes Course participants would be the recipients of deep and meaningful learning experiences.

The leader's role is to create a learning climate that offers challenges, fun, and success. S/he must also structure the situation to meet the predetermined goals of the program. To lead participants into an activity without this may result in haphazard learning or none at all. A processor, facilitator, or leader, must then be flexible, and respond with intuition and emotion, at appropriate times, as the situation warrants it. These skills are developed over many years, through awareness, internalizing experiences and continuous self-evaluation and improvement. Be willing to do what you are asking others to do.

Processing emphasizes how to utilize past experiences in making future decisions, and therefore how to direct or alter future behaviors, and thus, achieve desired results. Learning resulting from experience is of greater significance than the nature of the experience itself. Processing, or debriefing, after the activity gives the participants an arena for discussion and integration of the experience. This art of systematic questioning and analyzing of an event leads the participants to greater self-awareness, and assists them in applying lessons learned to other situations. To leave without processing the experience could negate the good that has been accomplished.

Participants come to your Ropes Course for many different reasons. To be effective as a facilitator you need to have a clear understanding of both individual and group goals. Talking about goals during the early stages of your experience helps set the tone for the day as well as clarifying the day's focus. This can be especially helpful in dispelling any myths, disbeliefs, or exaggerations of what a Ropes Course day can accomplish. If individuals or groups arrive at your course with expectations that it will change personalities, resolve long-term grievances, or act as a cure-all, they (and you!) will have a long and unsuccessful day. This is not to say that experiences don't change people and they sometimes change personalities, but it is to say that in order to best facilitate a day, you need to know what your clients are looking for and expecting.

Giving individuals an opportunity to reflect on and articulate their goals is a very important part of the day. As a facilitator, this process helps to chart your course as well as helps to establish limits and boundaries for the day. The Ropes Course is often a very powerful experience and can tend to open up a lot of areas for participants. Having a clear sense of where the group wants to stay focused gives you a place to return to, a home to revisit. The depth of your processing is determined by the combination of the goals of your clients and your facilitation skills and training. If the group is there to have safe fun, try new things, and get to know each other, then the depth of your processing should correlate with these goals.

Because processing is more of an art than a science, no exact formulas can be set nor guarantees can be made that your questioning will always stay

Notes

within the confines of the established goals. A simple question in your mind may be a very complex and deep question to a participant. Learning how to bring forth just the right open-ended question and re-focus the group's energy and direction are great skills to master. It can be very tempting for a new facilitator to ask questions that are too deep, or challenge the participants to a level that is not appropriate. This is unfair and unethical to your clients and yourself. It is your responsibility to set and clarify personal boundaries by questioning and inventorying yourself.

You should never bring participants to a place from which you are not qualified to bring them back. As a facilitator, know your limitations and honor them.

Remember that you can't do it for them. Often, this is a learning experience for both participant and facilitator. Provide them with the opportunities to seek, and you become the supportive shadow. Never believe that you have all the answers.

A good staff member *must* develop the skill and ability to process effectively. Such ability comes with practice and continues to evolve over many years. Every new situation will offer new insight to the facilitator who seeks it. The most fundamental key to all good processing is a sense of deep caring and concern for our fellow beings.

These can be difficult skills to teach. Questions and techniques can be taught, but feeling and intuition develop with practice. A facilitator must also be able, once the safe learning climate is created, to ask the right question, accurately read verbal and nonverbal human response, and to be able to respond to both the here and now and also on a broader developmental level.

Be willing to take a risk.

Risk

To laugh is to risk appearing the fool.

To weep is to risk appearing sentimental.

To reach for another is to risk involvement.

To expose your ideas, your dreams, before a crowd is to risk their loss.

To love is to risk not being loved in return.

To live is to risk dying.

To believe is to risk failure.

But risks must be taken, because the greatest hazard in life is to risk nothing.

They may avoid suffering and sorrow, but they cannot learn, feel, change, grow, love, live.

Chained by their attitudes, they are slaves; they have forfeited their freedom.

Only a person who risks is free.

Anonymous

Processing Levels

Two Levels of Facilitation

According to Schwarz (1994), facilitation can be divided into two types, basic and developmental. These two types of facilitation are based on the objectives of the group. In basic facilitation, the group seeks only to solve an immediate problem, such as crossing a field of Boiling Peanut Butter or getting everyone on an All Aboard. The group uses the facilitator to temporarily improve its process. This type focuses on the here and now aspect of processing. When the group has solved its problem, the facilitation objective has been solved, even though the group may not have necessarily improved the effectiveness of its process. If the group has another problem to be solved, it will rely on the facilitator once again. This is a situation many new facilitators encounter, as they often provide too much information, remain too involved in the group process, have difficulty separating themselves from the group, or do not allow adequate processing time.

In developmental facilitation, the group seeks to improve its long-term process in addition to solving the problem. The group views the facilitator as someone from whom they can learn to improve their process. The group then applies its newly developed skills to solve its problem. When the group has accomplished its objectives, it will—as in basic facilitation—have solved its problem. But just as important, the group will have improved its ability to manage its process. If the group has another problem to be solved, it will be far less likely to rely on its facilitator because it has learned to improve the group process. This type goes beyond the here-and-now and extends into a long-term process.

Facilitator Roles

The roles for the facilitator are much different for the two types of facilitation. In basic facilitation, the group expects the facilitator to guide the process using what s/he knows about group process. In developmental facilitation, members expect to monitor and guide the group's process and expect the facilitator to teach them how to accomplish this goal.

Types of Intervention

Intervention is different for these types of facilitation. A basic facilitator intervenes when the group's process or other factors affecting the group interfere with its accomplishing specific and substantive goals.

A developmental facilitator intervenes under the same conditions as a basic facilitator. In addition, as a developmental facilitator s/he intervenes when the group's process or other factors affecting the group hinder the group's long-term effectiveness. S/he also intervenes when reflecting on the process would help members develop their processing skills.

Schwarz, Roger M., 1994. *The Skilled Facilitator*. San Francisco: Jossey-Bass.

Processing by Way of the Experiential Learning Cycle

Figure 7-1. A Version of the Experiential Learning Cycle

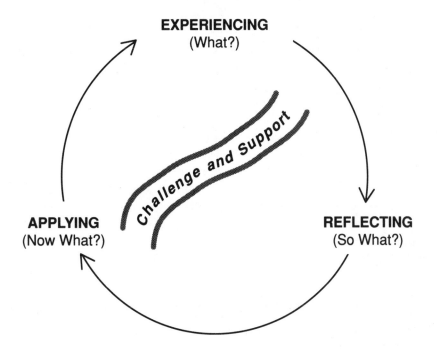

Figure 7-1: This diagram is a combination of ideas taken from the foundational thinkers of John Dewey, James Coleman, and J. Kirkpatrick. L. B. Sharpe and Julian Smith took this information and applied it to outdoor education concepts. Many leaders in student development, such as Kurt Lewin, have utilized this model in the creation of theoretical frameworks within their discipline.

The cycle has its roots in the century old belief of John Dewey that "all genuine education comes from experience." More recently people like Richard Kraft, Horwood, and J. Williamson have clarified the process and developed models similar to the one you see above. The word "experience" comes from the Latin word "experientia," meaning trial, proof, or experiment. Thus, the Ropes Course experience could be described as trial and error experiments that produce learning. There is immense learning potential hidden in Ropes Course activities. As facilitators we offer the necessary skills to help participants achieve learning.

There are many versions of the Experiential Learning Cycle. The words may vary, some use reflection, some use processing, and some envision a split in the application area—real life vs. simulated experience. Two central concepts—Challenge and Support—can be credited to leaders within the student development field. These two themes play a major part in helping participants move through the cycle and gain insight and experience. Participants have an inherent desire to learn and grow and by using these elements facilitators can be a catalyst for their change.

Although simple in appearance, we have found the experiential learning cycle to be very useful in helping direct participants in experiencing a more beneficial, meaningful day on the Ropes Course. We suggest describing this model during the opening stages of your Ropes Course and using it as a framework in processing initiatives and elements. Modeling this format will help ensure that participants receive the full impact of the day. We've found that while initially participants may be awkward with this process; it soon becomes part of the element itself. The group takes over the role of monitoring and guiding the cycle along.

If you are not intentional in your outcomes, the Ropes Course is just a series of games and activities without depth or meaning. Actually, the lack of intentionality is one of the larger stones that is thrown at our field. We need to be well and eloquently versed in what the experience can (and can't) provide to our participants.

Here is an example of using the cycle with a familiar low course event, the Nitro Crossing.

Experiencing (What?): Facilitators explain the challenge and objectives clearly, giving specific pointers for effective spotting and demonstration if appropriate. Facilitators get a clear contract with the group to accept the challenge. The group performs the activity. Facilitators observe passively, watching especially for safety. Facilitators call time (or they've completed the event) and the group stops the activity.

After the element (Experiencing), circle the group together and have them begin to reflect on their experience (Reflecting). Reflection is a critical piece of the cycle and unfortunately is one that is too often neglected.

Reflecting (So What?): Facilitators help the group members discuss their feelings and reactions toward the activity and one another that may have occurred during the element. Group members summarize their learning experiences about themselves and the team. Reflection can be an individual or group practice. Reflection can also take place verbally or by having participants engage in some form of non-verbal reflection, such as writing. Some of us do our best work (reflection) outwardly in action while others do their best work (reflection) internally. Don't rely solely on one format of reflecting.

By asking challenging and reflective questions and allowing for adequate processing, facilitators coach participants to discover their own answers. Reflection, in this particular case, involves the participant taking the Nitro Crossing experience from the outside world, bringing it inside his/her mind, turning it over, making connections to other experiences, and then filtering it through his/her personal biases. Even though the action was external (Nitro Crossing), and processing may have occurred within the group setting, the reflection occurs within the conscious mental-self. A significant advantage in having participants share their experiences is that other group members can relate this information to their own experience and help in their individual learning.

This learning experience can be accomplished through the description of the event, by looking at the stages they went through, by describing the feelings they experienced (what did they notice about the Nitro Crossing element?), group interactions, mistakes, etc. Generally, the reflection begins with specific examples and details. The other segment of reflecting involves generalizing, focusing on broader concepts and addressing the bigger question of "So What?".

Applying (Now What?): Hopefully, the reflection process brings about learning that will apply to the external world and that might just be different from the approach they normally would have used if reflection had not occurred. Participants will take this learning to other events (basic) or incorporate it into their lives in general (developmental).

Before you move on to another element, discuss what learning you will take from the Nitro Crossing to the next challenge (i.e. better communication, sense of humor, working together), and what you will leave behind (i.e. interrupting each other, not including everyone in decisions) in order to reach the groups goals and issues.

A good working knowledge of the experiential learning cycle combined with ample opportunity to practice will make a significant difference in what you and your participants derive from your day. Remember, the more you talk, the more the conversation will focus on you instead of the group. When a group gets accustomed to immediate feedback and discussion of cognitions and feelings, it evolves into a team more quickly. Another important aid for improving experiential learning is to get participants to "own" their cognitions and feelings by using "I" statements. Foster these practices, and you will be guaranteed to have a more open and highly energized group.

You will notice a big difference in how the group changes and develops throughout the day. A good working knowledge of group development can be very helpful in understanding the stages your group will experience.

Experiential Learning Cycle

A Model of Ropes Course Group Development

A group on the Ropes Course can take a variety of forms. You may be working with a group of at-risk adolescents, college freshmen, teenage girl scouts, or corporate executives. But, regardless of your group's population, one thing all groups have in common is that they are dynamic.

The group of people that you welcome to your Ropes Course in the morning will not be the same group you say good-bye to at the end of the day. Knowing and understanding how groups form and develop is critical in understanding how to sequence your day as well as "read" your group. Bruce W. Tuckman, a leading group dynamics theorist, developed five stages of group development (Tuckman 1965; Tuckman & Jensen 1977). His model is based on the successive stage theory of group development; it specifies the usual order of the phases of group development.

The five stages of group development
1. **Forming (Orientation)**
2. **Storming (Conflict)**
3. **Norming (Cohesion)**
4. **Performing (Performance)**
5. **Adjourning (Dissolution)**

Naturally, this series of stages will not apply to every group nor will every group experience each stage on the Ropes Course. It is, however, a very helpful tool to help understand the seemingly complicated and difficult patterns that can emerge throughout your program. According to Tuckman, each stage serves as a building block for the next and thus serves as a very important piece of the process. What follows is an expanded description of Tuckman's five stages of group development, potential observations, and applications within a Ropes Course context.

1. **Forming:** During the initial stages of your Ropes Course, the group members are trying to get to know each other, determining the "why" of their presence, exploring personalities and relationships, and increasing their interdependence. A strong reliance on the facilitator for information and advice is typical at this stage. This stage is generally seen during the warm-up games, ice-breakers, and early initiatives during which tentative conversation is shared, ideas are coached in a guarded manner, and generally individuals are "feeling" each other out.
2. **Storming:** As your group progresses into higher level initiatives and low-course elements, you may begin to see individuals voicing strong beliefs, sharing differences of opinions, disagreeing over ways of doing things, and some resistance to the process. A natural consequence of all groups is disagreement. This stage is one that may cause many participants a great deal of anxiety and uneasiness if they do not understand the basic nature of group development or the potential benefits of conflict.
3. **Norming:** After the group has progressed through the storming stage, it begins to develop cohesiveness and should begin to grow closer.

Members begin to develop roles, establish their own rules and procedures, and watch out for each other. During an element you may notice that they are supporting each other's ideas, really listening to each other, and gaining respect and trust.

4. **Performing:** After the group has had a variety of experiences and opportunities to work together, they may reach this stage in which they become much more task focused and clearly defined. According to Bales, task-focused actions occur more frequently later in the group's life (Borgatta & Bales 1953). Very few groups are productive immediately, they must wait until they mature before they become productive. Much of the productive behavior that occurs in the early part of the day may be mistaken for the performing stage; however, if the group has not progressed through the earlier stages, it has not yet reached this stage. An example of this stage would be when the group arrives at an initiative, discusses their ideas and options, comes up with a plan, they all agree, and then they begin to tackle the challenge. The absence of dissent, disagreement, and excessive discussion, and the presence of teamwork, flexibility and clear communication are all typical at this stage. Remember that not all Ropes Course groups will reach this stage. Sufficient time is needed for the group to reach this level, though time alone is no guarantee.

5. **Adjourning:** A group may enter this stage by either a *planned* or *spontaneous* route (Forsyth, 1993). The day may have a planned dissolution when it reaches its goals or exhausts its time or resources. This is very different from a spontaneous dissolution that may end when an unanticipated problem arises that ends the day, i.e. weather, emergency. This stage can be a stressful one for participants. After all, breaking up is a hard thing to do. Facilitators can do much to help ease the tension that can arise during this stage. Planning an appropriate and realistic schedule, keeping on "track," ensuring participants have been able to process their experience throughout the day, all helps to reduce the pressure of the end. Providing participants with an opportunity to reach closure is a must! Ensure participants have a voice and an ear during the final activity. Make sure you have a planned closing activity in mind that will include all participants.

Borgatta, E. F., & Bales, R. F. (1953). Task and accumulation of experience as factors in the interaction of small groups. *Sociometry*, 16, 239–252.

Forsyth, Donelson R. (1993). *Group Dynamics*, 2nd ed. Pacific Grove, California: Brooks/Cole.

Tuckman, B. W. (1965). Developmental sequences in small groups. *Psychological Bulletin*, 63, 384–399.

Tuckman, B. W., & Jensen, M. A. C. (1977). Stages of small group development revised. *Group and Organizational Studies*, 2, 419–427.

Notes

Facilitator Characteristics

*"Who you are speaks so loudly
I can't hear what you're saying."*
Ralph Waldo Emerson

Facilitators play a primary role in the successful outcome of a Ropes Course experience. The facilitator's function is to create a safe and supportive environment that encourages exploration, risk taking, and personal growth. The following characteristics of a facilitator will ensure more meaningful outcomes for Ropes Course participants.

- Good listening skills

- Non-judgmental stance

- Focused

- Technically proficient

- Organized and on time

- Patient

- Knowledgeable and safe

- Observant

- Casually competent

- Mentally and physically fit

- Willing to learn and grow

- Genuine

- Good sense of humor

- Team player

- Articulate and professional

- Positively assertive

- Open and friendly

- Huge sense of playful fun

Commitment Agreement

No idea is stupid, that is offered conscientiously.

Direct confrontations away from others.

Be a good peer example.

Do not use offensive language.

Talk to participants at their level.

Challenge by choice—choose to do "something."

Be a leader *not a* boss.

Listen and support each other.

Laugh with—not at.

Don't gripe, whine, or complain.

Respect each other's opinion, don't interrupt them.

Accept and offer constructive criticism.

Criticize behavior, not the person.

Respect all staff, be attentive.

Don't discount this commitment.

Notes

Useful Beliefs about People on the Ropes Course

- As a facilitator, your communication influences the response you get from participants.

  It is your responsibility to find a way for participants to learn and grow. If they don't respond at first, try a new approach. Often changing your language or using examples, metaphors, or analogies, can bring new meaning to the participants.

- The most useful information that we have is behaviorally specific.

  You can tell more about what a person really means by observing *how* s/he communicates (nonverbally), than you can from just listening to what s/he says. "No way" seldom means no way.

  A continual nonverbal, behavioral dialogue is happening within your group. Your job is to pay close enough attention to the signals, and accurately express or modify your activities, in order to create the most meaningful experience for the participants.

- Mind and body affect each other.

  If someone is stuck in a negative emotion, have them shift his/her body, or attention, and notice what happens. Move people around, and you help shift their perspective.

- We are *not* our behaviors.

  A participant says: "I'm afraid of heights."

  Facilitator: "Yes, you've had some past experiences that cause you to behave fearfully. What would happen if you were able to manage this situation so that you . . ."

- Our present behavior is the best choice available.

  Even if a person is acting unproductively, at some level this is the best way that s/he knows how to deal with the current situation.

  Acknowledge and respect the fact that participants are acting the best way they know how. You could then ask, "If there was a way for you to experience this safely, without those feelings getting in the way, would that be of value to you?" Break the experience down into smaller, more manageable steps. Success comes from taking steps, regardless of their size.

- Behavior is geared toward adaptation.

  People adapt their behaviors to match their current beliefs about what is possible or not possible in their lives. When their beliefs expand, their behaviors automatically adjust to reflect their new beliefs.

Your job is to open the door of possibility and to offer them an opportunity to walk through this door. Often, people don't realize they they have a choice. *Remember, the choice is theirs.*

- Every behavior has a place, or situation, in which it is appropriate.

Before you cast judgment on someone else, remember that even seemingly unproductive behavior (such as freaking out) has a place and a function in that person's life.

Your role is to assist participants in finding eloquent ways to express their true needs. Your ultimate goal is for participants to discover more choices, which then lead to greater flexibility and confidence in dealing with any given situation.

- We have all the resources that we need.

Remember, people are not broken or in need of being fixed. What they require is a way to access the internal resources that they already have, and to find a way to transfer these to a given task.

If a person says "*I can't do that,*" your job is to find a time from her/his past when s/he felt competent at doing something, and have her/him pretend s/he feels the same way now. You can actually help transfer these feelings and beliefs, and this will assist her/him in behaving more resourcefully in this new situation.

As a facilitator, by offering participants a combination of challenges and support, we help facilitate growth and contribute to a meaningful and long lasting experience.

Notes

Processing Issues and Related Questions

"If you treat an individual . . . as if he were what he ought to be and could be, he will become what he ought to be and could be."
Goethe

The following questions are ones that the authors have had success with in processing Ropes Course experiences. You will develop your repertoire of questions as you continue to gain experience and insight. We encourage you to record your favorite questions in the open areas we've provided in each section.

Opening
- What are you hoping for from today's experience?
- What kind of support do you need from the other group members?
- What do you perceive will be difficult for you today?
- What excites you about the Ropes Course?
- What can you offer the group today?
- Knowing your typical role in a group, what role would you consider assuming today?
- What are your personal and group goals for the day?
- What kind of support do you need from the facilitators?
-
-

General
- What happened that you liked or disliked?
- What contributed to the group's success?
- What would be helpful to change in order to be successful with future events?
- What did you discover about yourself? The group?
- How did you decide how you would do the element?
- Who knew the plan?
- How did you handle leadership?
- How do you handle fear?
- In what ways can you *apply* what you have learned?
-
-

Communication
- What did you ask for from the group?
- What prevented you from asking for what you wanted or needed?
- What was helpful or disappointing about your style of communication?
- What differences did you notice about other group members' styles of communication?
- What was confusing about a person's style of communication?
- Who was included in the flow of communication? Excluded?
- Whose suggestions were listened to? Ignored?
- Whose suggestions were acted on? Ignored?

- In what ways did the communication pattern change throughout the day?
- In what ways can you *apply* what you have learned?
-
-

Decision Making/Problem Solving

- What *is* the problem?
- What are the most important concerns you have about the problem?
- What are some of your lesser concerns?
- What are some other solutions? Brainstorm them.
- What is the best alternative for you? The group?
- What did you discover when you re-evaluated your choice?
- What changes do you need to make?
- What, or who, was helpful in solving the problem?
- What, or who, was a hindrance in solving the problem?
- How do you typically solve a problem? Make a decision?
- In what ways can you *apply* what you have learned?
-
-

Trust

- What makes it difficult to trust? Yourself? Others?
- What behaviors and attitudes help you build trust?
- What behaviors and attitudes get in the way of building trust?
- Which role is easier, the one trusting or being trusted?
- Which role is more difficult, the one trusting or being trusted?
- How would the group act, or look, if we were trusting?
- What can you do to help increase the trust level in the group?
- In what ways can you *apply* what you have learned?
-
-

Expression of Feelings

- How are you feeling right now? Consider mad, glad, sad, and scared.
- Describe one feeling that you have experienced today. What was going on?
- What were some of the feelings that came up for you today?
- What feelings are the easiest to express?
- What feelings are the most difficult to express?
- Were the ways you expressed your feelings today, typical or atypical, of how you usually express them? If atypical, how do you usually express your feelings?
- What feelings did you notice that the others were expressing?
- What feelings were hardest to be around?
- What feelings were expressed nonverbally today? Describe how they were expressed?
- What feelings did you keep inside today?
- What feelings do you want to keep most fresh in your memories?
- In what ways can you *apply* what you have learned?

Notes

-
-

Individual Differences

- In what ways are the group members similar? Different?
- How did the differences within the group prove to be a strength?
- How did the differences within the group prove to be a hindrance?
- How are you different from some of the group members?
- How did your differences affect the group?
- What stereotypes became apparent within the group?
- What was the basis for any of the stereotypes?
- What societal stereotypes were challenged today?
- How could the group learn and benefit from individual differences?
- In what ways can you apply what you have learned?
-
-

Individual Responsibility Taking

- What can you do, specifically, to make a difference?
- Name three things that you want others to know, or ways that you'd like them to act differently?
- How much control did you have today? Others?
- What makes it seem that others have more control than you?
- What personal attitudes and behaviors could you change, or influence change in others, for the day?
- What prevents the group from using "I" statements?
- What changes need to be made to avoid attacking or challenging certain behaviors within the group?
- In what ways can you apply what you have learned?
-
-

Team Work

- Specifically, how did your group work together?
- Specifically, how did your group make decisions?
- In what ways was your group cooperative? Give examples.
- In what ways was your group uncooperative? Give examples.
- What strengths were evident in your group? Weaknesses?
- What contributed to the success of your group?
- What prevented your group from being successful?
- What role did you play within your group?
- What did you appreciate about your group? Individuals?
- What strengths did you offer to your group?
- How does the group measure success? How do you?
- In what ways can you apply what you have learned?
-
-

Closing

- What were your goals at the beginning of the day?
- What goals were you able to meet? Not able to meet?
- What did you learn about yourself today? The group?
- What specific memories, or visuals, will you take away from today's experience?
- Who did you really appreciate or enjoy today? Give specific examples.
- What are you most proud of from today's activities?
- What specifically was fun about today?
- In what ways was your behavior today typical, or atypical, of how you usually act in groups?
- In what specific ways will you apply what you learned from today's experience?
-
-

Handling Difficult Situations

As a facilitator, you will encounter many challenging situations during a Ropes Course experience. We have outlined some suggestions for dealing with a few of these difficult situations. This is not intended to be an inclusive list. With increased experience and confidence, you will develop your own techniques.

Silent Co-Facilitator

Do:

Make sure you divide up responsibilities for the day.

Ask "What's up?". Talk to the person.

Acknowledge that the person is quiet (especially if they are quieter than usual).

Get in the habit of asking the person "Is there anything you'd like to add?" or "What do you think?"

When dividing up responsibilities, make sure they are comfortable with their assignments.

Keep up with them during the day, i.e. maintain good eye contact or when on the high course, yell up "How are you doing?"

Give them many openings to comment on certain things; this also takes some pressure off of you.

When you debrief the day, make sure it is a two-way conversation. Offer feedback to him/her.

Don't:

Ignore that they are being silent.

Be exclusive and talk "about" them.

Push them aggressively to speak up, especially in front of participants.

Be a monopolizing facilitator to compensate for them.

Lack of Cooperation Among Facilitators

Do:

Respect each other.

Have a "team plan."

Support each other.

Be flexible.

Communicate positively.

Spend "enough" time processing your day.

"Do unto others as you would have them do unto you."

Don't:

Have a confrontation in front of the group.

Overpower the co-facilitator.

Judge your co-facilitator.

Put the group in an uncomfortable position by forcing them to take sides or in any other way, be affected by your "stuff."

Non-inclusive Spirit in the Group—gender, size, culture, personality, etc.

Do:

Make alliances by showing connections or similarities between people.

Purposefully get people with differences to interact.

Be sensitive to different "strengths" or "roles" on initiatives.

Use blindfold exercise (or eyes closed) to establish trust and increase understanding.

Challenge gender (or other) stereotypes, ask "Why?".

Know your group composition before the day, plan accordingly.

Use your influence as a role model.

Maintain a diverse staff on your Ropes Course.

Practice inclusive language.

Don't:

Stereotype on basis of gender, size, culture, etc.

Make generalizations about your participants.

Allow one facilitator to seem more important, knowledgeable, or somehow "better."

Ignore the non-inclusive spirit.

Proceed too quickly or react too quickly.

Lack of Team Building Spirit in the Group

Do:

Review initial individual and group goals.

Choose initiatives and games to build team spirit.

Process during the activity and focus on the team.

Consider appointing a "leader" for activities.

Know your group ahead of time. What experiences have they had together?

Don't:

Ignore the lack of team building spirit.

Feed into it or encourage competitiveness.

Single one person out or embarrass someone.

Lose your composure.

Unsuccessful Effort by the Group

Do:

Look at why it's not working, ask the group and ask yourself.

Re-focus.

Break the task down into smaller, more manageable steps.

Consider offering them hints, i.e. non-verbals, helping statements, talking them through it—"Have you used all your resources?"

Use analogies or metaphors.

Re-define success.

Re-frame success.

Encourage participation.

Praise effort.

Don't:

Always stop the group when unsuccessful.

Use negative terms.

Give them the answer.

Lecture.

Take it personal.

Assume there is only one right way.

Assume that there aren't any major learning's in "Failing Forward."

Group Member Makes Disrespectful Comments

Do:

Mentally review whose issue it is—review full-value contract.

Evaluate the impact on group member.

Re-evaluate sequence to see if the group needs to do another initiative/ game to develop trust and respect.

Don't:

Single out either party.

Ignore the situation.

Let it grow.

Let it influence you and the others.

Let it hinder your abilities as a facilitator.

Judge.

Participant Refuses to Participate (not fear-related)

Do:

Listen and realize their limits.

Be emphatic, not sympathetic.

Keep group focused on goals.

Be flexible.

Check in with person to see if s/he is willing to share with group the reason for not participating.

Acknowledge her/his role and importance to the group.

Remember "Challenge by Choice."

Don't:

Laugh.

Ostracize.

Humiliate.

Stop activity.

Blow out of proportion.

"Holler" at the person.

Fearful Participant

Do:

Be sensitive to feelings.

Make alliances by connecting with withdrawn or fearful participant.

Remember "Challenge by Choice."

Encourage participant to say "I choose not to . . . right now" instead of "I can't."

Break goals down into easily accomplished tasks.

Balance encouragement with limit setting.

Smile, use tension breakers (i.e. yell, make faces, breathe!).

Create win/win situations.

Unobtrusively encourage communications.

With care, ask them to be a leader for an element.

Don't:

Draw attention to her/his face.

Allow participants to say "I can't."

Over facilitate to compensate.

Set participant up for failure.

Create competition or comparisons.

Single them out.

Give them "too" much attention.

Wait until it is too late to deal with the situation.

Assume that participants need to "do it all" in order to have a successful experience.

Nervous and Anxious Participant

Do:

Reassure and comfort them.

Ask what they need.

Reinforce positives.

Offer choices and options.

Use "Challenge by Choice" appropriately.

Reflect.

Trust the process.

Find the "good" in the person's choice.

Don't:

Ignore.

Say it's okay.

Use pressure—
  time pressure.
  peer pressure.
  participant pressure.

Single out people.

Stray from goals.

Try to make it better.

Don't bring in facilitator's "stuff."

The "Jokester" Participant

Do:

Laugh with and not at them.

Deal with him/her tactfully.

Talk about how that might affect others feelings.

Equalize the situation so they don't need to crack jokes in order to be accepted.

Notes

Return to the original goals.

Find other acceptable ways of releasing tension.

Stop and re-evaluate.

Re-focus.

Re-direct.

Consider using your quiet voice—change your approach.

Renegotiate group goals, if needed.

Remain patient and calm.

Don't:

Encourage the behavior.

Retaliate or try to "get even."

Give them ammunition.

Discourage having fun, unless it is negative.

Embarrass.

Judge.

Divide group into "good and bad."

Move on until group is ready.

Loose your cool!!

The Advice-Giving Participant

Do:

Acknowledge good advice.

Reinforce the emphasis on teamwork.

Move quickly to next point.

Give encouragement to try out a different role.

Acknowledge the importance of other roles, not just being a verbal leader.

If the problem becomes too severe: discreetly speak with person alone; add challenges to elements in order to help them; control the urge to contribute excessively.

Quickly recognize the problem and take action.

Don't:

Ignore what they have to offer to the group.

Let them stifle or control the group.

Verbally attack them out of frustration.

Wait to address the problem.

Monopolizing Participant

Do:

Handle the issue directly and with tact.

Take advantage of "trail talk"—pull them aside and talk with them on the way to the next element.

Stand next to that person in the circle.

Watch for safety problems that could arise.

Go back to the goals of the day.

Ask directly for involvement of others, i.e. "Can we hear from some other participants?"

When soliciting input, go around the circle to ensure everyone has a voice.

Ask the group if everyone is being heard.

Don't:

Ignore the situation.

Condone the situation.

Allow it to divert the group from its goals.

Expect the group to handle it on its own.

Resort to sarcasm or embarrassing the participant.

Silent or Withdrawn Participant

Do:

Pay attention to body language.

Include a silent or non-verbal activity.

Ensure the s/he is physically in the group.

Enforce the "no double parking" rule in the group.

Notes

Go around the circle when looking for input.

Use her/his name when talking to participants.

Choose activities that must include everyone.

Have acceptable roles for everyone.

Walk and talk with them between elements.

Gently prompt them to speak, especially when you see them having a "Ahh Ha" experience.

Make sure you talk about the benefit of trying out new roles.

Encourage them not to go last.

Accept that they are quiet and may not want it differently.

Ask for someone who has not spoken.

Ask if there is anyone who would like to share, then wait.

Don't:

Be "too" obvious with your intentions.

Embarrass them or make them feel weird.

Allow them to exclude themselves from the group.

Allow it to divert you from your primary goals.

Create situations that force them to stand out, i.e. put them in the middle or make them a leader.

Assume you know why they aren't talking.

Take it personal.

Chapter 8

Elements

"You don't need a high ropes course to offer an effective adventure experience." KER

A high ropes course . . .
. . . is a big budget item.
. . . requires special and intensive training to facilitate effectively and safely.
. . . slows participation via a series of high element bottlenecks.
. . . requires consistent and comparatively expensive maintenance.
. . . is at the least an insurance hassle and at the extreme a program ending liability disaster.

Having cathartically fulfilled my current less-is-more philosophy relating to adventure programming, I would also like to pass along that a ropes course . . .
. . . provides an effective and dramatic tool toward self discovery.
. . . is extremely effective toward developing one-on-one trust.
. . . is a ropes and cabled garden of useful metaphors.
. . . is flat-out the most fun and excitement you can legally and morally experience with a group of just-met strangers.
. . . provides an unforgettable, high profile experience that has relevance and carry over to a participant's daily life.

The point(s) I'm trying to make is that if your recently funded grant allows $15,000 toward implementing an adventure program, don't immediately spend the farm on a high ropes course. A high course is unquestionably a useful facility toward achieving program goals including trust, self esteem and mutual respect, but—start slowly. Use some of that available cash for acquiring simple props (game bag contents) and training, training in how best to use those experiential toys, but most importantly how to facilitate the adventure experience. Then spend a sizable chunk of the remaining dinero to have a few *low* ropes course elements installed, also to include (as above) associated training to insure effective and safe use. Finally, put enough aside for a couple high elements; emphasizing again the necessary training.

Not to beat a dead horse or batter you with metaphors, but . . .

Your most essential budget item is training.

Adventure programming is not purely academic, sports oriented or recreational, rather a unique and pedagogically solid emphasis on experiential hands-on learning. What's that mean? Buy the training, it's the best learning bang you'll ever get for your educational buck, and you won't have to listen to me anymore.

Karl's Games and Initiatives Reference List

Top Tricks

Karl Rohnke

Key to Source Books[1]		Key to Activity Use	
BBA	Bottomless Bag Again!?	OutdoorActivity	O
BB	Bottomless Baggie	Indoor Activity	I
SB	Silver Bullets	Indoor/Outdoor	I/O
CT&C	Cowstails & Cobras II	Activity Level High	S (sweat)
BOTs	Bag of Tricks	Activity Level Medium	MS
QS	QuickSilver	Activity Level Low	NS
FS1	Funn Stuff #1		
MAN	Not Published		

No Props

Add On Tag	O	S	BBA-81	SB-42	
Ah-So-Ko	I/O	NS	FS1		
"Bang . . ."	I/O	NS	BBA-45		
Bends, The	I/O	MS	QS-240		
Blind Fold Line Up	I/O	NS	BBA-98		
Bottoms Up	I/O	MS	CT&C-39	BBA-6	SB-159
Bumpity-Bump-Bump	I/O	MS	BBA-9	QS-84	
Categories	I/O	NS	BBA-143	QS-85	
Caught Ya Peekin'	I/O	NS	BBA-125		
Chronological Line Up	I/O	NS	SB-163		
Circle Slap	I	MS	FS1		
Co-op. Comp.	I/O	MS	BBA-5	SB-94	
Coming and Going of the Rain	I/O	MS	SB-92		
Commons	I	MS	QS-110		
Count Off: 1–20	I/O	NS	BB-179	BBA-95	
Diminishing Load	I/O	S	SB-138		

---

[1]All of the above books can be ordered from Kendall/Hunt Publishing Co. Call the following number to order or for information: 1-800-228-0810.

Dog Shake	I/O	MS	SB-168	CT&C-36	BBA-15
Elbow Tag	I/O	S	BBA-2		
Everybody Up	I/O	MS	CT&C-39	BBA-96	SB-100
Everybody's IT	I/O	S	BBA-1		
FFEACH	I/O	MS	QS-114		
Gooney Likes . . .	I	NS	BBA-125		
Gooney Variations	I	NS	QS-251		
Hands Down	I	NS	BBA-46	SB-53	
Hog Call	I/O	MS	SB-98	WS-202	
Hopping	I/O	S	CT&C-30-33		
Hospital Tag	I/O	S	BBA-2	*See* Sore Spot Tag	
How're Ya Doin . . .?	I/O	NS	BBA-51		
Human Camera	O	NS	BBA-18		
Hustle Handle (Hustle Bustle)	I/O	NS	BB-96	CT&C-66	QS-87
"I Trust You, but . . ."	I	MS	BBA-15	SB-91	
Impulse Genre	I/O	MS	BBA-141	CT&C-69	
Inch Worm	I/O	MS	SB-158	CT&C-38	BBA-150
Invisible Jump Rope	I/O	S	SB-157	BBA-7	
It Ain't Me Babe	I	NS	QS-80		
I've Got The Beat	I	NS	BBA-47		
Killer	I/O	MS	SB-52		
King/Queen Me	I/O	MS	QS-245		
Knee Slap	I/O	NS	BB-1	QS-246	
Monster	I/O	S	SB-132		
Mrs. O'Grady	I/O	NS	BBA-153	SB-180	
Name Tag	I/O	MS	QS-207		
Pairs Squared	I/O	S	QS-90		
Pairs Tag	I/O	S	BBA-2		
Passing Xed . . .	I	NS	BBA-47	SB-55	
PDQ Test	I	NS	SB-172	BBA-151	
Popsicle Push Up	I/O	MS	SB-166	BBA-96	
Quick Line Up	I/O	S	QS-182		
Red Baron	I/O	MS	CT&C-37		
Retro-Eknhor	I	NS	BBA-9		
Return to the Earth	O	NS	CT&C-41		
Reversing Pyramid	I/O	NS	BBA-95		

Sardines	I	NS	SB-30		
Sherpa Walk	O	MS	BBA-16	SB-87	
Sore Spot Tag	I/O	S	BBA-2	*See* Hospital Tag	
Speed Rabbit	I/O	MS	BBA-91	CT&C-63	
Squat Thrust	I/O	MS	SB-94	MAN	
Striker	I/O	S	BBA-88	QS-135	
Subway Sardines	I/O	MS	*See* Trust Circle		
Tangle (Knots, Hands)	I/O	MS	NP	SB-117	*See* Buddy Ropes
Team Tag Tag	I/O	S	BBA-4		
Texas Big Foot	I/O	MS	SB-46	BBA-25	
The Clock	I/O	S	SB-116		
Trust Circle	I/O	MS	QS-233		
Trust Wave	I/O	MS	QS-234		
Twizzle	I/O	S	QS-137		
2 x 4	I/O	NS	SB-123		
Where in the Circle Am I?	I/O	NS	QS-92		
Whizzzz Bang	I/O	MS	QS-141		
Yeah, but	I/O	MS	SB-91		
Yell	I/O	NS	CT&C-45		
Your Add	I/O	NS	BBA-48		
Zombie	I/O	NS	QS-144		

Medium Props

Acronyms	I	NS	BB-16	FS1	
Alienation	I/O	NS	QS-98		
All Catch	I/O	NS	BBA-80	BB-2	
Almost Infinite Cir.	I/O	NS	SB-131		
Ankle Biters	I/O	S	BBA-78		
Asteroids	I/O	S	BBA-77		
Auto Tag	I/O	S	QS-100		
Back Stabbers	I/O	S	QS-101		
Balance Broom	I/O	MS	SB-164	CT&C-44	

Balloon Frantic	I	S	BBA-66	SB-19	
Balloon Trolleys	I	MS	QS-149		
Bean Bag Tag	I/O	S	QS-103		
Blind Polygon	I/O	NS	CT&C-81		
Blindfold Soccer	I/O	S	SB-69		
Body Sac	I/O	MS	BB-28	BBA-27	
Boffer Bonkers	I	S	BBA-73		
Booop	I	MS	SB-49	BBA-67	
Buddy Ropes	I/O	NS	BB-46	QS-220	
Bugs in my Cup . . .	I	NS	FS1		
Catch 10	O	S	SB-64		
Claydoughnary	I	NS	QS-109		
Compass Walk	O	MS	SB-176		
Cranial Snatch It	I/O	MS	BB-69		
Dollar Drop	I/O	NS	QS-238		
Dollar Jump	I/O	NS	SB-174	BBA-31	
Don't Touch Me!	I/O	MS	QS-156		
F Words	I	NS	BBA-124		
Fast Draw	O	MS	SB-28	BBA-30	
Fire-In-The-Hole	I	MS	SB-51	BBA-67	QS-199
Group Juggling	I/O	MS	SB-112	CT&C-84	QS-201
Heads & Tails Tag	I/O	S	BBA-6	QS-91	*See* Transformer Tag
Hooper	O	S	BBA-79		
Monarch	O	S	BB-13	QS-125	
Moonball	I/O	MS	SB-31	BBA-56 BB-14 & 104	CT&C-60 QS-176 & 206
No. 10 Tin-Can Foot Pass	O	MS	BBA-117		
Nuclear Fence	I/O	MS	BB-100	QS-208	
Orange Teeth	I/O	NS	BBA-41	SB-147	
Samurai Challenge	I/O	MS	SB-45	BBA-75	
Toss-A-Name-Game	I/O	NS	SB-17	BBA-8	
Touch My Can	I/O	NS	BBA-115		
Warp Speed	I/O	MS	CT&C-83	BBA-53	
Whoo . . .?	O	NS	SB-73	BBA-82	
Wordles	I	NS	SB-102	BBA-120	

Props

Amazon	O	MS	SB-137		
Amoeba	I/O	NS	FS3-27		
Balloon Stack	I	NS	FS3-41		
Balls Galore	I/O	NS	SB-175		
Bottom Line	I/O	MS	BB-15		
Bridge It	I	NS	SB-127	BBA-112	
Bump	I/O	MS	SB-68		
The Button Factory	I/O	MS	FS2-2		
Circle The Circle	I/O	MS	BBA-115	SB-60	
Climb All Over Me	I/O	MS	FS2-27		
Cold Shoulder	O	S	FS3-47		
Comet Ball Boccie	O	MS	QS-241		
Comet Balls	O	MS	BBA-68	SB-25	BB-90 QS-242
Commandant	O	S	SB-73	BBA-81	
Croc Pit	O	S	FS3-42		
Cucaracha	O	S	FS3-7		
Dangle Duo Double Use	I/O	MS	QS-197		
Disc Jockeys	I/O	MS	BBA-226		
Do-I-Go	I/O	MS	BBA-227	QS-154	
Duct Tape	I/O	MS	FS2-38		
Flip Me The Bird Tag	I/O	S	SB-155	BBA-3	
Flip Side	I/O	MS	FS3-37		
Frantic	I	S	SB-18	BBA-65	
Frog Wars	I	S	BBA-84		
Funnelator	O	MS	BBA-146		
Gotcha	I/O	NS	FS2-3		
Great Egg Drop	I/O	NS	BBA-111		
Half Pipe	I/O	MS	FS2-19		
Hammeroids	I	NS	QS-162		
Hansel & Gretel	O	NS	QS-200		
Have You Ever . . .?	I	NS/ MS	BBA-127	BB-93	QS-224
Help Me, Rhonda	I	NSI	BBA-45		
How We Differ	I	NS	QS-77		
Human Ladder	I/O	MS	BBA-14	SB-113	

Human Overhand	I/O	NS	FS1		
Hut, 2, 3, 4 . . .	I/O	MS	FS2-21		
In & Out	I	S	BBA-56		
Is This It?	I	NS	BB-52		
Italian Golf	O	MS	BBA-86	CT&C-67	
Jumping Jack Flash	I/O	S	QS-167	*See* Hop Box	
Junk Yard	O	NS	BB-49	QS-168	
Kangaroo Catch	O	MS	QS-121		
Key Punch	I/O	S	QS-169		
Knot A Knot	I/O	MS	FS3-2		
Le Cav	I	NS	FS2-16		
Leaning Tower of Feetza	I/O	MS	FS2-22		
Left Person/Right Person	I/O	MS	FS3-11		
Maze	O	NS	QS-203 & 232		
Metamorphose	I/O	MS	FS2-12		
Mine Field	I/O	NS	BBA-52	QS-148 & 205	
Nesting Balls	I/O	S	BOTs-62		
Nutsy	O	NS	BB-90		
Object Retrieval	O	MS	BBA-110		
Onion Jousting	I/O	MS	BBA-90	QS-178	
Paper Chute	I	NS	QS-179		
Pauls Balls Box	I/O	MS	SB-21	BBA-109	
Peek-A-Who	I/O	NS	BBA-10		
Phones & Faxes	I/O	MS	SB-63		
Pick & Choose	I	S	SB-77	BBA-51	
Ping Pong Pyramids	I	NS	QS-181		
Polar Bears . . .	I	NS	BBA-101		
Porcupine Progressions	I	NS	BBA-102		
Pot-A-Gold	I/O	S	FS3-13		
Raccoon Rings	I/O	MS	BOTs-62		
Ready Aim . . .	O	MS	QS-131		
Ricochet	O	MS	QS-133		
Rodeo Throw	I	S	BBA-33		
Rolling Raft Adventure	I	S	BBA-107		
Rope Push	I/O	S	BBA-40		

Scooter Slalom	I	S	SB-66	BBA-37	
Shark	O	S	SB-47	BBA-59	
Shoot Out	O	S	SB-39	BBA-61	
Single Line Potpourri	I/O	MS	BBA-186		
Snow Flake	I	NS	SB-145	BBA-39	
Speedy Gonzalez	O	S	MAN		
Spider Web	I/O	MS	SB-114	QS-209	
Spotting Gauntlet	I/O	MS	FS2-35		
Squirm	I/O	S	BBA-33		
Stepping Stones	I/O	MS	BBA-105	QS-186	
Swat Tag	I/O	S	BB-95		
Tangrams	I	NS	SB-129		
Tattoo	I	S	SB-22		
The Wave	I	S	BBA-88		
This Is Bocce?	O	MS	FS3-19		
Touch & Go	I/O	NS	FS3-5		
TP Shuffle & Sprint	O	MS	QS-212		
Traffic Jam	I	NS	SB-122	QS-211	
Trolley	O	S	SB-118	BBA-221	QS-214
Trust Fall/Dive	I/O	NS	BBA-19	SB-80	CT&C-53
Tubecide	O	S	SB-70		
Turnstile	I/O	S	BBA-116	SB-156	*See* Hop Box
Tusker	O	S	SB-42		
Twirlies	I/O	MS	QS-256		
Two-In-A-Row	I/O	S	BBA-116		
Unholy Alliance	O	S	SB-36	BBA-57	
Up Chuck	O	MS	BB-2	BBA-80	QS-191
Up Nelson	I	NS	QS-257		
Waiter Wars	O	S	QS-139		
Wallets	I/O	NS	FS2-29		
Waumpum	I/O	NS	BBA-10		
Whale Watch	O	NS	QS-192		
Wiggle Waggle	I/O	NS	FS3-61		
You Tear Me Up	I	NS	QS-238		FS3-30
Yurt Rope	O	MS	QS-258		

Index of Low and High Course Elements

Generic High Ropes Course Considerations

Technical Aspects

Each high Ropes Course element involves a specific set up and procedural requirement. The following need-to-know considerations are included here as a generic list to avoid a repetitive listing below.

- String a section of 9 millimeter slash rope between two trees or poles at about chest level. Use this line to suspend all carabiners and belay devices. This is done to keep the gear organized and clean.
- Flake or spaghetti your belay rope to check its integrity.
- Use the #4 nylon cord (lazy line) to raise and reeve the belay rope into place.
- Check that all the rescue and first aid kits are on the site.
- Check that all helmets on site are clean, sizable, and functional.
- All Studebaker wraps and harnesses should be checked before climbing.
- All knots checked by the instructors and by one another.
- Check all carabiners to be sure they are screwed down, not up.

High Course Individual and Group Issues

- The high course is primarily an individual challenge.
- One suggestion is to require participants to pair up (and one triad if numbers are uneven) in order to offer support and clear communication with their partner(s). This works especially well with static courses as they can literally be up there together helping each other succeed.
- Participants can also communicate to the group about the way in which they would like support (quiet or boisterous).
- Fear of heights
- Trust in themselves and equipment
- Self-confidence and esteem
- Letting go, control

Sequencing of Events

- In order to ensure participants and groups have a meaningful experience from the high course, they need to experience the low course.
- Based on the individual, some elements may be harder or easier.
- The Pamper Pole and the Zip Line are two of the most difficult high course elements.
- Two easier elements are the Cat Walk and Burma Bridge.

High Ropes Course Elements

Pamper Pole

Objective and Description:
- To jump (dive) from the top of an erect utility pole or tree platform in order to grab a trapeze (or touch some hanging object). The climb to the top is made on staples driven into the tree or pole. The belay rope runs through a shear reduction device attached to an overhead belay cable.

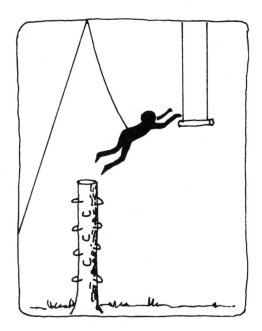

Figure 8-1. Pamper Pole.

Specifications:
- Two parallel 3/8 inch GACs strung between two trees or poles 20 to 30 feet apart. The top cable is the belay cable and the bottom cable is the one with the trapeze, bell or ring being suspended from it. The belay cable is usually 30 to 36 inches above the bottom cable. The pole is usually positioned five to seven feet back from the cables and is in the middle of the two support poles. A Jus-rite belay log is highly recommended on this element.

How to Set Up:
- Use the in-place lazy line to set up the belay rope.
- Clip a locking D carabiner through the bowline-on-a-bight tied into the end of the belay rope. Clip that carabiner through the back of a Studebaker wrap. If a combination Studebaker/chest harness is used, the entire double loop of the bowline-on-a-bight is clipped into the chest and pelvic harnesses with two carabiners—one carabiner into the chest harness and one carabiner into the pelvic wrap.
- The belayer uses either a sticht plate-type belay device or reeves the belay rope through a Jus-rite descender.

Time and Group Size:

- Once the Pamper Pole element is "opened" the group's attention will center on that activity. Don't allow this event to control what you are trying to accomplish with your group.
- If a person on top of the pole has been agonizing about making the jump for over five minutes, strongly suggest that person needs to make a decision about continuing or descending. Challenge by choice certainly, but it's time to make that choice *now*.
- This exciting event is a huge bottle neck. You will be fortunate to get 6–8 people to complete this event in a class block or 45 minutes.

Rules and Safety Concerns:

- Obese participants or those people with odd body shapes should be required to wear a full body harness or a combination of chest harness and pelvic wrap.
- Depending upon the relationship of the element's height and "give" in relation to the belay supports, people over 250 pounds should be encouraged not to make the climb. The 250 pound figure is somewhat arbitrary. To know for sure on your course, drop an on-belay 250 pound weight (not a person) from the top of the entry ladder (the ladder used to achieve the first climbing staple). If the weight slams into the ground on full belay, rethink that poundage figure.

Flying Squirrel

Objective and Description:

- Participation on this event allows a physically challenged or extremely fearful participant to experience trust and control of fear.
- A participant (even someone in a wheelchair) is hauled, via a static rope and pulley, to maximum height on a ropes course by 10–15 other members of the group.
- A participant can choose from one of two "rides" or a combination of both. The first is a simple hauled ride to the top. The second alternative is "flying," which involves a running-cum-pendulum movement by the rider.

Specifications:

- Use a length of 3/8 inch GAC suspended between two trees or poles approximately 20 to 25 feet apart. The cable should have at least a four to six foot center drop, and should be backed-up like a belay cable. In the middle of the cable is a five to six inch sheave, backed-up rope pulley. A static 1/2 inch kernmantle rope is strung through the pulley with an in-place lazy line. On one end of the rope, a bowline-on-a-bight, is attached to a full body harness with a locking carabiner bight. The other end of the rope is tied into a bowline-on-a-bight with each bight loop attached individually to two participants. The other ten participants hold and pull the rope without attachment.
- Use an industrial rated (sealed bearings, minimum 1/2 inch axle, aluminum sheave) single wheel pulley.
- Use a short length of double eye-spliced cable as a back-up device.
- 12 millimeter kernmantle KM111 is the static haul rope of choice. Do not use dynamic climbing rope for this activity.

- Use a full body harness or a combination pelvic wrap/chest harness for each participant.
- When taking someone up in a wheelchair, harness the participant and tie in the chair separately from the participant.

How to Set Up:
- Use the in-place lazy line to set up the belay rope.
- Clip a locking D carabiner through the bowline-on-a-bight tied into the end of the belay rope. Clip that carabiner in the rear connection loop of a full body harness.
- At least ten participants act as the haulers with two of them attached to the end of the rope, as mentioned in specifications section.

Time and Group Size:
- This is an element that most people want to try, and it is, therefore, time consuming.
- A minimum of ten people should be considered as pullers for this element. Very heavy people will require up to 15 pullers.

Rules and Safety Concerns:
- A person should not be pulled directly to the top, but be offered a chance to make a choice (keep going, let me down) at various stages along the way.
- Do not allow "flying" if there is a chance that the participant can hit a solid object "in flight."
- Do not pull a participant all the way to the top so that their knotted static rope strikes the pulley.
- Develop commands for this event that allow an unequivocal response and understanding by everyone, climber, pullers, and facilitator alike.

Cat Walk

Objective and Description:
- A log or utility pole supported horizontally between two trees or poles.
- To walk across the horizontal log.
- To attempt the passage backwards, with eyes closed, hopping, or jogging—your choice.
- To hang off the bottom of the log and then try to regain a position on top of the log. This is very difficult.

Specifications:
- If a natural log is used, it should have all the bark peeled off before installation. After a couple weeks this allows for the application, of a wood preservative.
- A utility pole may be used (approximately 30 foot Class IV) suspended between two support trees or Class II poles, and parallel to the ground. Connection to the tree supports should be such that the trees are not being girdled.
- A belay cable parallels the log at about eight to ten feet above the log, beyond the reach of the participant. The log is supported by 5/16 inch or 3/8 inch GAC. Four to six 1/2 inch or 5/8 inch SLES are used to

support the cable and to protect the support trees. The log should be hung in manner that allows at least four to five years of growth without constricting or otherwise damaging the tree. The support cable can be wrapped around the log or passed through a 5/8" bolt placed in the log.

How to Set Up:
- Use a single wheeled cable pulley with two quick links, or two locking carabiners, connecting the single pulley to the spin static pulley. See Figure 2-37. Reeve the belay rope through the spin static and tie a bowline-on-a-bight in the end. The belayer would use a belay device to belay the participant. Clip a carabiner onto the bowline-on-a-bight and attach the carabiner into the participant's harness.

Time and Group Size:
- It will take approximately 1.5 hours to get 12–15 participants through this element. Be sure to plan for debriefing in addition to this time frame.

Rules and Safety Concerns:
- Try to convince the log walkers to make their crossing without holding onto the belay rope.
- If a participant falls, the belayer should initially let out enough rope to allow the climber to fall below the log, not into the log.

Multi-vine

Objective and Description:
- Attempting to traverse the foot cable by using only the sequentially hung vine-like ropes.
- The horizontal foot cable should be as taut as the supports allow.
- The "vine" ropes should be so sequenced that moving from rope to rope is not possible without making a lunging motion i.e. briefly free of both ropes.

Figure 8-2. Multi-vine.

Specifications:
- Three parallel 3/8 inch GACs, tautly strung between two trees or poles, making the lower cable the foot cable, middle cable has four to five multiline ropes vertically hung for support, top cable (backed up)

as belay. The middle cable is attached by NEB and back-up strand vises or cable clamps set so that the cable does not tangle with the top or belay cable. The vine ropes are hung at varying distances apart depending on the length of the vine ropes, size of population and the designed level of difficulty. Cable drops are acceptable for vine rope attachments.

- Use 5/8 inch diameter hawser-lay multiline rope to fabricate the "vines."
- Sequence the ropes to provide a realistic challenge. This will vary as to the length of the cable, the length of the "vine" ropes, and the abilities of your student population.

How to Set Up:
- The belay cable and "vine" support cable need to be installed parallel to one another and as far apart as possible to allow the belay pulley to roll unobstructed.
- A rear participant clip-in functions best with this event.
- Use the same belay set-up as described for the Cat Walk.

Time and Group Size:
- It will take approximately 1.5 hours to get 12–15 participants through this element. Be sure to plan for debriefing in addition to this time frame.

Rules and Safety Concerns:
- The belayer should be so positioned as to keep the ascending and descending slingshot belay ropes away from the grasp of the participants.
- In the event of a lunging fall, the belayer should allow the student to fall below the foot cable to prevent injury.

Heebie Jeebie (Pirate's Crossing)

Objective and Description:
- To cross from one support tree to another via the fabrication of descending and ascending ropes on cable.
- Sections of 5/8 inch diameter multiline rope are connected from supports to a horizontal foot cable. The rope/cable connection distance is approximately 2/3 of the way across the cable from the rope initiation point.

Figure 8-3. Heebie Jeebie (Pirate's Crossing).

Notes

Specifications:
- Two diagonally crossing multivine ropes (1/2 inch multiline minimum, 5/8 inch preferred) are connected from the poles to the taut traverse footcable (3/8 inch GAC), at points which are two thirds the distance from the poles, forming a quasi-hourglass shape. The preferred method of attaching the ropes to the foot cable is via rapid link in thimbled eyesplice connected to cable with cable clamp; rapid link "u," (saddle up on cable), and nuts tightened to maximum torque. Bolted rapid links should be angled toward the appropriate tree. The rope/tree attachment choices are 1/2 inch protection staple, 1/2 inch SLES, or 5/8 inch SLES. After the placement of rope/tree attachment, the rope end is reeved through the staple or SLES and tied off in a prusik, tightened, and the excess rope taped or eye-and-backspliced into the working end so that it still feeds through the staple freely to facilitate tautness. A belay cable (3/8 inch GAC) runs approximately ten feet above and parallel to the foot cable.

How to Set Up:
- Front harness clip-in works best on this element.
- Although unlikely, be prepared for a rescue on this event. A student can get irretrievably tangled among the belay rope and crossing ropes and cable.
- Use the same belay set-up as described for the Cat Walk.

Time and Group Size:
- It will take approximately two hours to get 12–15 participants through this element. Be sure to plan for debriefing in addition to this time frame.

Rules and Safety Concerns:
- See above about tangling. Be aware that this can occur and try to talk students out of making movements that will allow this to happen.
- The belayer should stay opposite the climber as much as possible to prevent a pendulum fall and possible contact with the supports.

Two Line Bridge (Postman's Walk)

Objective and Description:
- A relatively simple traverse crossing on cables that involves maintaining foot contact with the bottom cable and hand contact on the chest-high cable.
- A third cable is strung horizontally overhead as a belay cable. This cable should be high enough to preclude the climber from reaching up and grabbing the shear reduction belay device and/or pulley.

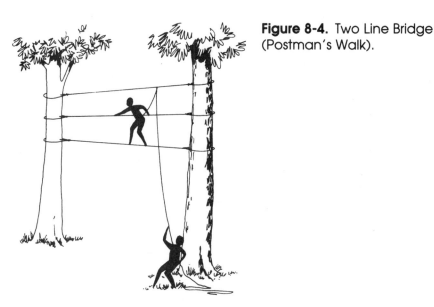

Figure 8-4. Two Line Bridge (Postman's Walk).

Specifications:
- Three parallel GAC's strung between two trees or poles. The top cable is the belay cable. The middle cable acts as a hand line; the bottom cable is stood and traversed upon. The distance between the bottom and middle cable is determined by the average height of the student population but averages between 32 to 48 inches. Make sure the belay cable is installed high enough so that a participant standing on the bottom cable cannot reach up and grab the top cable, or the shear reduction device.

How to Set Up:
- Use the same belay set-up as described for the Cat Walk.

Time and Group Size:
- If static belays are being used, quite a few people can be encouraged through this simple crossing.
- Remember not to put more than two belays on a belay cable.
- It will take approximately 1.5 hours to get 12–15 participants through this element. Be sure to plan for debriefing in addition to this time frame.

Rules and Safety Concerns:
- If a participant wants to detach mid-crossing, either: (1) Allow enough slack rope so that the student will fall below the cable. (2) Ask the student to keep their feet on the bottom cable, grab their own belay rope, and let go of the hand cable. You can then slowly lower the student until their feet detach from the cable, by which time they will pendulum below the cable.

Burma Bridge

The *Burma Bridge* is just a fancy *Two Line Bridge*. Most Burmas are now constructed without "herring bone" crossing ropes, which can cause problems with retrieving the belay rope.

Notes

Figure 8-5. Burma Bridge.

Zip Line

Objective and Description:
- To descend from a high Ropes Course event by rolling down an inclined cable on a two wheel pulley. The rider is connected between a seat harness and the pulley by a section of double eye-spliced rope.
- Braking is achieved by use of a bungee cord or by establishing a caternary (dip) in the cable as to achieve a gravity braking effect.

Figure 8-6. Zip Line.

This figure depicts an out-of-date braking device. Current zip lines are built using a gravity brake.

Specifications:
- A 3/8 inch GAC attached between two poles or trees usually between 250 to 400 feet apart. The cable is strung in a sagging fashion with the middle of the cable far enough from the ground so when the heaviest participant is attached, at that point her/his feet are at least three feet from the ground. The participant is attached to an acceptable two wheeled pulley which rides on the cable. The participant is stopped with either a gravity brake or a brake block. Both ends of the cable should be backed up in an acceptable manner. Both bolts should be drilled and set at a 35 degree downward angle depending on the anticipated drop.
- A double wheel pulley is desired because of the straight tracking benefits and the extra safety achieved by having two wheel axles.
- The wheels (sheaves) should be milled steel, never aluminum.
- The angle of descent and height of the take off platform are variables that should be estimated and implemented by Ropes Course builders, experts concerning the dynamics of zip line construction.

How to Set Up:
- The rider should descend with a front clip-in, unless the bottom of the caternary is high enough to allow the use of a full body harness.

- A facilitator should be on the platform to remove the climbing belay, attach the pulley, and provide some needed emotional support or encouragement.

Time and Group Size:
- There is no way to make this a quick event, and indeed there is no reason that it needs to be accomplished rapidly. However, things can be approached efficiently by making sure that the next climber is ready to go as soon as the first climber is on the platform and off the belay.
- The is usually a "final" event, so emphasize enjoyment.

Rules and Safety Concerns:
- If you are the facilitator on the platform, make sure that the rider is completely detached from the platform (no connector ropes) before initiating the ride.
- If a length of bungee cord is being used as the braking device, be sure that the cord is not being "maxed out" by the riders. A rebounding broken cord can inflict substantial personal damage.
- Injuries occur too often while the rider is detaching and descending from the step ladder. Be sure that the descending team knows what it is doing.

Dangle Duo

Objective and Description:
- For one or two climbers to ascend the cable supported parallel beams in order to achieve standing or sitting (whichever seems most appropriate) on the top beam. The cable side supports cannot be used for support or climbing.

Specifications:
- A vertically oriented five rung beam ladder suspended from an overhead cable. Beams are usually eight foot pressure treated 4 x 4s. The distance between the first two rungs is generally 4.5 feet and increases by 3–4 inches, rung to rung. A separate belay cable (backed-up) is suspended above the uppermost log.
- The rungs appear equidistant from the ground but actually differ by 3–4 inches per section.
- Longer and wider rungs can be used to allow up to four climbers to ascend simultaneously.
- If more than two climbers are going to be on the element, two separate belay cables are necessary.
- An 18 inch section of 1/2 inch diameter PVC pipe can be slid onto the belay cable before installation in order to keep the two belay shear reduction devices from juxtaposing (getting mixed up).

How to Set Up:
- Double the Cat Walk belay set-up or attach spin static directly to cable with one steel locking "D" carabiner. Ensure the carabiner is locked with gate screwed down.

Time and Group Size:
- Six people are involved if two people climb; two climbers, two belayers, and two back-up belayers or, two climbers and four Australian back-up belayers.
- Climbers regularly take 30–45 minutes on this event.

Rules and Safety Concerns:
- When the climbers are ready to descend, attach a short section of rope to the bottom rung and pull it away from the belayers. This keeps the climbers from bouncing off the rungs during their descent.
- Climbers should not try to use their belay ropes for support, nor use the cables.

Hour Glass

Objective and Description:
- Traversing crossed lengths of 3/4 inch multiline rope between two support trees or poles.
- The object is to make the crossing between the trees or the poles by using only the crossed ropes to avoid contact with the ground.

Specifications:
- The top anchor staples are driven at seven feet above the bottom staple.
- Connectors between rope and staple can be either rapid links or carabiners. The crabs require less time for attachment.
- A prusik loop in each rope allows for occasional tightening of the event, or conventional removal.

How to Set Up:
- Use the same belay set-up as described for the Cat Walk.

Time and Group Size:
- It will take approximately two hours to get 12–15 participants through this element. Be sure to plan for debriefing in addition to this time frame.

Rules and Safety Concerns:
- There is only one participant on the ropes at a time. Falls are frequent and occur suddenly. If a facilitator is on static belay, he/she should be prepared to assist or rescue the participant.

Low Ropes Course Elements

Trust Fall

Objective and Description:
- To perform a controlled fall from a four foot high platform into the arms of at least eight arranged spotters.
- The platform can be built on a pole or tree or the facilitator can choose other convenient flat areas to initiate the fall.

Figure 8-7. Trust Fall.

Specifications:
- Wooden platform measuring usually 24" x 32". Made of 2" x 6" (frame) and 2" x 10" (top) pressure treated lumber. Frame is bolted together with 1/2 inch stove bolts and aircraft nut and washer. Top may be attached to frame with 16D galvanized ring-shank nails, or #10 3 1/2 inch deck screws. Attached with eight 6" x 1/2" galvanized lag screws. Average height is 40 inches above ground in spotters area.

How to Set Up:
- Ask for a volunteer—form two parallel lines facing each other, directly in line with the platform. Spotter's arms should be in an "L" position with legs apart—one about two feet in front of the other. Knees bent. Heads back.

Time and Group Size:
- Plan on 30–45 minutes. Minimum of 8–10 participants, maximum of 16–18.

Rules and Safety Concerns:
- All sharp objects and loose jewelry should be removed before participating.
- Ensure the catchers rotate throughout the line so individuals don't always catch the torso.
- Make sure that the participants are positioned appropriately to best catch faller, i.e. stronger people to catch larger people.
- Require that the following commands should *always* be used:

Participant:	Group ready?
Group:	Ready. (Stated with conviction)
Participant:	Trusting?
Group:	Trust Away. (Stated with conviction)

Notes

- After participant falls, ensure group stands him/her up and cradles them until they regain their footing.

Individual and Group Issues:
- Emotional and physical trust
- Clear and assertive communication
- Gender and body image
- Focus

Example Processing Questions:
- What role was easier, the one trusting or being trusted?
- In what ways were you able to ask for what you wanted?

Sequencing of Event:
- This event would come well into the day after such events as Blind Trust Walk, Tic Toc, Willow-in-the-Wind, Minefield, Web.
- You could follow this event with the Wall, Hickory Jump, or more intense and involved problem-solving initiatives.

The Wall

Objective and Description:
- To move the entire group as efficiently as possible up and over the Wall. The Wall itself is a 12 foot high obstacle that varies in width. One side is blank (the side to be climbed). The other side has a railed platform to stand on, and a means of descent (usually a ladder or staples).

Figure 8-8. The Wall.

Specifications:
- A smooth surfaced wall, 12 foot high, eight to ten feet in width, nailed to four 4" x 4" (minimum) cross supports (decay-resistant lumber). If the wall is placed on poles, the minimum depth of placement is four feet without external support. The top 4" x 4" should be attached with through-bolts to prevent lag bolt breakage. The face of the wall may be two inch stock treated lumber, six inch to ten inch in width and fastened the same as the surface of the platforms. The bottom of the face of the wall should start two feet from the ground level. A permanent deck should be attached approximately 36 inches in width, running the entire length of the wall. The deck will be nailed to three vertical

4" x 4"'s, the same height as the top of the wall, should be held secure by a minimum of two feet in the ground. The surface of the deck should be approximately 42 inches from the top of the wall. A 2" x 8" treated board, lag screwed with 3/8" x 3 1/2".

- The height of the Wall can vary as to the age and performance capability of the group. The width of the Wall should be such that a sense of challenge is promoted.
- Staples should be driven into one of the supports to allow participants to descend, or use a ladder.

How to Set Up:
- Check the ladder and tie it off if it is removable.

Time and Group Size:
- This initiative problem can be attempted for some time, but in most cases this approach is contraindicated because of the increased chance of injury.
- The ideal group size is somewhere around 12, allowing everyone a chance to participate and be heard.
- As far as scheduling time, allow 20–25 minutes.

Rules and Safety Concerns:
- No one should end up in a position where their head is below their feet. This prevents hanging someone over the Wall upside down.
- The Wall is "infinitely" wide, so the sides of the Wall do not exist and therefore cannot be used in the ascent.
- After a person has gone over the Wall and has come down on the far side, that person cannot provide physical aid to other climbers. Those people can and should act as spotters. Spotters are needed on the front and back of the Wall, and also should be located laterally on the front of the Wall during ascent.
- All sharp objects and loose jewelry should be removed before participating.
- Three people are allowed on top with one in the process of climbing the Wall. If there are four participants on top, one must descend.

Individual and Group Issues:
- Perceived and actual strength
- Individual and group problem-solving
- Appropriate touching
- Persistence, stick-to-it-ness!!

Example Processing Questions:
- What stereotypes became apparent within the group?
- How do you typically react to frustrating activities and/or people?

Sequencing of Event:
- This is a powerful end of the day event, make sure that the group is demonstrating effective communication and trust. Also make sure that the group has enough energy and physical stamina to be potentially successful. This could come after an intense problem-solving initiative or trust fall.

Notes

- This event can be the end of a low-course segment and may be followed by preparation toward the high-course.

Spider's Web

Objective and Description:
- A "spider's web" configuration is easily fabricated between two trees, poles, standards, etc.
- The object is to move the entire group through the web openings so that each person goes through a distinct opening without touching the web. If a participant is successful, that opening conceptually closes for the remainder of the problem.
- If anyone touches the web during an attempt, the person being passed through must return and try again through that same opening.

Figure 8-9. Spider's Web.

- The web is made up of tied sections of 3/16 inch bungee cord as to simulate an ersatz (substitute) spider's web.

Specifications:
- A customized, fabricated web strung between two trees or poles usually 10 to 12 feet apart. The web should have 12 to 20 holes sizable for participants to move through. The web border is made of 1/2 inch multiline rope, the interior of the web is made of 3/16 inch bungee or a combination of bungee and 1/8 inch rope. The top of the web will be no more than six feet in height. The web can be constructed to be removed by using screw eyes or staples in the tree or poles. The web should be attached by clips on the web.

How to Set Up:
- This initiative problem can be made easily portable. When you take down the web, lay it on a bed sheet and roll it up as is. When it's time to use the web again, simply unroll the sheet.

Time and Group Size:
- This initiative does not lend itself to being timed.
- If the group numbers more than 20 people, two separate webs should be utilized. These two webs can be positioned in such a way as to form an "open book." With a group of 20, allow 25–30 minutes.

Rules and Safety Concerns:
- The web measures approximately eight feet long by six feet high and consists of about 14–20 web openings.
- If a participant is being guided through a web opening, they should be passed through head first and face up so that efficient spotting of the head is possible.
- Each person being passed through an opening should be spotted the entire time that they are off the ground.
- At least two participants should step through a lower web opening before anyone is lifted so that they will be on the far side to protect the people being passed.

Individual and Group Issues:
- Appropriate touching
- Gender issues
- Trust
- Effective communication
- Setting boundaries
- Body image

Example Processing Questions:
- What specific attitudes and behaviors make it difficult to trust others?
- What made it difficult (or easy) to allow others to lift you?

Sequencing of Event:
- The group needs to have had experienced events involving appropriate touching, such as People-to-People or Human Knot. The group also needs to have practiced lifting events, such as Cookie Machine, and Levitation.
- This activity could be followed by the Trust Fall, or a culminating event such as the Wall.

Wild Woozey

Objective and Description:
- Two diverging cables that originate from the same support and are connected on the far end into two separate supports, approximately 12–14 feet apart. These taut cables are about 18 inches above the ground.
- The object is for two participants, each standing on a separate cable, to maintain physical contact with one another and move from the apex of the traverse to the far end without falling from the cables or losing contact.

Figure 8-10. Wild Woozey.

Specifications:
- Two tautly stretched 3/8 inch 7 x 19 GAC approximately 18 inches in height and starting at the same point, progress outward to end points approximately 12 feet apart.

How to Set Up:
- Provide the participants a 20 inch section of two inch diameter PVC pipe. Indicate that they can use this pipe section in any way they wish, but that the PVC cannot make contact with the cables or ground. (Utilize the pipe as a hand held object to lean against to take the pressure off wrists and fingers. Other uses prove to be a waste of time.)
- Ask spotters to be available when the two participants begin leaning toward one another.

Time and Group Size:
- This is not a timed event.
- Indicate to the group that getting two connected people to the end of the event should be thought of as a group goal. Everyone should be thinking and working together toward this goal.
- Allow 20–25 minutes for a group of 12–16.

Rules and Safety Concerns:
- Two spotters should stand behind the two participants as they begin. This is a shaky precarious time on the cable.
- As the two cable walkers begin leaning toward one another, spotters beneath the extended bodies will become necessary. These spotters should lean forward with their hands and arms in an "L" shape positioned beneath the participants (like a Trust Fall). Start with one spotter and by the time the walkers are well separated, up to six side-by-side spotters may be necessary.

Individual and Group Issues:
- Trust in self and partner
- Communication
- Challenging gender stereotypes
- Gender and size issues
- Balance—personally and physically

Example Processing Questions:
- What influenced your choice of a partner?
- How does "balance" play a role in your life?

Sequencing of Event:
- Before this element be sure to practice spotting and do some activities that utilize verbal commands.
- This element could be a part of a trust sequence.

TP (Telephone Pole) Shuffle

Objective and Description:
- Place your entire group on top of the horizontal pole. Divide the group in half and ask those two halves to face one another and trade ends without stepping off the pole, or making contact with the ground.
- The pole is usually a 30 foot utility pole supported a few inches off the ground by two or three supports.

Specifications:
- A 30 foot section of telephone pole (or hardwood log) is bolted atop, or pinned with 5/8 inch bolts, to the two notched log crosspieces. Average height is 12 to 18 inches to the top of the log.

How to Set Up:
- An alternative use is called *The TP Sprint*. In this case, divide the group in half and ask one half to stand at one end of the pole on the ground and for the other half to duplicate that positioning at the other end. Four members of the group should volunteer to be "facilitators." Their permanent position is anywhere *on* the log. Everyone is on the same team and is trying to achieve the following goal: for the groups to change ends as quickly and efficiently as possible without touching the ground.

Time and Group Size:
- This is ordinarily a timed event. As such, the objective should be attempted a second time so that the group can benefit from their first experience. Indicate that for each ground touch a 15-second penalty will be assessed.
- If there are more than 20 people on the pole this may become awkward.

Rules and Safety Concerns:
- This is a self spotted event: i.e., the participants should be aware that a fall to the ground is possible, and they should be responsible for themselves to stay on top, as well as for the members of their team.
- During *The TP Sprint*, members of the group will be jogging the length of the log. Alert the group to the possibility of a turned ankle and suggest to temper their enthusiasm with care.

Individual and Group Issues:
- Working together, communication, problem solving
- Physical balancing
- Appropriate touch

Example Processing Questions:
- What made this element challenging?
- What does it take to make this element succesful?

Sequencing of Event:
- This element can be an early or beginning initiative.
- You may follow this up with more complicated initiatives.

Mohawk Walk

Objective and Description:
- The "Walk" is made up of sections of taut cable between support trees; some long, some short. The group objective is to move all participants from one end of the event to the other via the taut cables.

Figure 8-11. Mohawk Walk.

Specifications:
- A series of five low cables tightly strung between trees or poles 18 inches above the ground, with a tension rope to provide a means of traversing the last cable. The cable is 3/8 inch 7 x 19 GAC (galvanized aircraft cable). All bolts are through bolted. No threaded screw-on thimble eye bolts. If these are on poles use at least Class III poles with anchors at each end.

Time and Group Size:
- Not a timed event.
- Completion of a multiple-stage Mohawk can often take a group of 15 participants over an hour.

How to Set Up:
- Mohawk Walks vary considerably in the number and the extent of the cable crossings. Be aware that different spotting stances will be necessary.
- Use of turnbuckles on each cable allows a convenient put up/take down capability for this and other low events.
- Connect traversing rope and check all cables and connections.

Rules and Safety Concerns:
- The facilitator, and all those participants not yet on the cables, should act as spotters. Spotting is very essential on this event.
- If a tension traverse, swing, or multi-vine is part of the crossing, make sure that at least one spotter is assigned to the person making the attempt.

Individual and Group Issues:
- Greater physical balance
- Resource utilization
- Making changes, movement, pathway

Example Processing Questions:
- What resources did you need to complete the element?
- What kind of support did it take to get across the element?

Sequencing of Event:
- Successfully complete an easier initiative first, i.e. Nitro Crossing, Web.
- This initiative allows participants to become familiar with cable walking which can be helpful for the high course.

Single Line Potpourri
1. **Nitro Crossing**
2. **Disc Jockeys**
3. **Do I Go?**
4. **Swing Aboard or Prouty's Landing**

Objective and Description:

1. Nitro Crossing
- Involves swinging the entire group across an open space (poisoned peanut butter, etc.), and then clearing a "trip wire" obstacle at each end of the swing.
- The intensity of the challenge can be increased by including a #10 tin can 3/4 or almost full of water (nitro) in the crossing.

Figure 8-12a. Nitro Crossing.

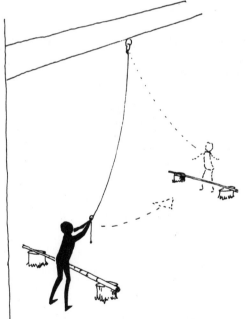

2. Disc Jockeys
- By utilizing the same swing rope, swing the entire group, person-by-person into a ground level pyramid of bicycle tires, located approximately where the *Swing Aboard* platform is located. Use one bicycle tire per student. **Note:** Hoola Hoops may be substituted for cycle tires.
- The objective is to fill the entire pyramid with students, one participant per tire. The pyramid's base should be facing the swingers.

• Only two feet are allowed in a tire. Three feet in a tire (no matter how temporary) requires that both people return to swing again.

Figure 8-12b. Disc Jockeys.

3. Do I Go?

• Using four *All Aboard* platforms placed equidistant from the swing's plum (imagine the number five on a di, where the swing is the center dot and the platforms are the four surrounding dots), ask the group to divide themselves equally onto the four platforms, then try to see how quickly it takes for each participant to end up on a different platform.

• The swing rope is obviously the only way to make the crossing from platform to platform.

• Do not allow more than four on a platform.

Figure 8-12c. Do I Go?

4. Swing Aboard or Prouty's Landing

• This is identical to the *Nitro Crossing* above, except that the far "trip wire" is replaced with a 3' x 3' platform. The object is to swing each participant onto that platform and maintain a balanced posture, with all aboard, for ten seconds.

• If anyone falls off the platform or touches the turf on the swing across, that person must return for another try.

- If the "trip wire" near the origin of the swing is knocked off, the entire group on the platform must return.

Figure 8-12d. Swing Aboard or Prouty's Landing.

Specifications:
- Drill through and place a 5/8" Nut Eye Bolt (NEB) in a substantial limb. Make sure this limb can withstand sustained shock load forces delivered by swinging bodies of up to 250 lbs. Eye splice one end (or tie a bowline knot) of a 5/8" diameter section of hawser laid rope (multiline). Using a 5/8" rapid link, clip the eye splice (knot) into the overhead NEB. Splice a generous loop in the dangling rope end or, again using a bowline knot, establish the loop. The bottom of the loop, when weighted, should hang about 10" off the ground.

Rules and Safety Concerns:
- Spotting is obviously essential during swinging events. Most of the spotting is the responsibility of the facilitator, but the participants should be aware enough not to attempt bizarre swinging positions.
- A loop should be spliced into the end of the swing rope to allow those students without requisite upper body strength to make the crossing. Foot-in-the-loop swingers usually require the most attention by spotters.

Individual and Group Issues:
- Trust
- High level problem-solving initiative
- Gender stereotyping—i.e. males assume greater expertise and finesse

Example Processing Questions:
- What assumptions did you hold at the beginning of the element?
- What did the group do to contribute to your trust level?
- How did you utilize your resources?

Sequencing of Event:
- This element is an early initiative, after ice-breakers, and warm-ups.

Triangular Tension Traverse

Objective and Description:
*   This low balance/trust element is made up of three taut cables strung between three support trees, with two ropes available for tension support. Turnbuckles can be used to vary the challenge or to entirely remove the cables.
*   Participants try to balance their way around the triangular traverse using a tension rope for support.

Figure 8-13. Triangular Tension Traverse.

Specifications:
*   3/8 inch GAC tautly strung in a triangular pattern approximately 18 inches above the ground, between three support trees. Two multiline ropes attached vertically to one apex tree for support of a participant traversing the cable.

How to Set Up:
*   The tension ropes connect to the dangling tension cables using a carabiner. Remove these ropes when the event is completed to prevent unauthorized use of this event.

Time and Group Size:
*   Schedule 30–35 minutes for a group of 12–16.

Rules and Safety Concerns:
*   Only two people can participate at the same time unless additional cables are installed.
*   Announce that each wire walker requires a minimum of four spotters. At least two of the spotters need to position themselves between the walker and the rope support to prevent the walker from penduluming back into the tree or into the ground.
*   Falls are frequent on this activity; spotters have to be attentive at all times.
*   Emphasize that the spotters are there to protect, not to maintain the person on the cable.

Individual and Group Issues:
*   Individual challenge with support from the group.

Example Processing Questions:
- What types of support worked best for you? What types of support hindered your progress?
- What part of the element proved most challenging for you?

Sequencing of Event:
- This element is an early initiative. Make sure the group is functioning well in spotting and commands.
- This element can be followed by the Mohawk Walk or Wild Woozey.

All Aboard

Objective and Description:
- To support as many people as possible on the platform (off the ground) for a measured ten seconds.
- The portable platform can be just about any dimension depending upon the size of the group. A 2' x 2' platform is the classic size and, with time and effort, can support 15–17 people.

Figure 8-14. All Aboard.

Specifications:
- At least a 2' x 2' platform made from two-inch thick pressure treated wood for the top and supported by two two-foot long 4" x 4"s. Galvanized 16D ring shank nails or #10 3 1/2 inch deck screws are to be used to attach the top boards. All lumber must be treated against decay. Maximum board spacing on top is 1/2 inch. Edges on the top must be rounded or beveled.

Rules and Safety Concerns:
- Do not allow the "Lincoln log" scenario (stacking participants) to develop. Students piled up in this fashion can cause serious injury to one another.
- If students choose to climb on each other, allow them to climb on their backs but not on their shoulders. Require spotting for the person at risk.

Individual and Group Issues:
- Appropriate touch
- Body size
- Effectively communicating ideas
- Problem-solving skills

Notes

Example Processing Questions:
- What assumptions did you hold at the beginning of the element?
- How did you know if you heard from all the members?
- What types of communication were at play during the element?

Sequencing of Event:
- Play games (i.e. People-to-People) that involve appropriate touch.
- This can be one of the first problem-solving initiatives.
- Use this non-threatening initiative to acclimate group to debriefing techniques and/or goals (i.e. experiential learning cycle).

Trolleys

Objective and Description:
- Using the provided props, to cross an "area of noxious material."
- The crossing props consist of 10–16 foot lengths of 4" x 4" lumber, with sequenced four foot sections of rope attached. The ropes can either be located every 12 inches along the length of the two boards, or located only at the ends of the boards (four ropes). This latter rope location causes more contact between participants.

Figure 8-15. Trolley.

How to Set Up:
- Establish the "noxious substance" area. Delineate this no-touch expanse with two lengths of slash rope, polyspots, or cones.

Time and Group Size:
- This can be a timed event, but applying penalties for slips off the log works well also.
- The group size is limited by the size of the 4" x 4". Rather than increasing the length of the boards, increase the number of boards available.
- Allow 20–25 minutes on your schedule for 12–14 people.

Rules and Safety Concerns:
- If someone falls off a board (either foot) that person must reverse their position (about face) on the board, or be assigned a time penalty.

Individual and Group Issues:
- Clear communication, including effective listening.
- Leadership concepts, such as communication across the lines, placement of leaders within a group, and assumptions about leaders and followers roles.

Example Processing Questions:
- How did you decide who would become the leader?

- How did you determine what role the leader would assume, i.e. calling cadence, being positioned up front.
- How did followers contribute to the success of the group? What role did they play?

Sequencing of Event:
- Play games (i.e. People-to-People) that involve appropriate touch.
- This can be one of the first problem-solving initiatives.
- Use this non-threatening initiative to acclimate group to debriefing techniques and/or goals (i.e. experiential learning cycle).

Whale Watch

Objective and Description:
- A 6' x 14' (dimensions can vary) platform placed on top of a fulcrum board to establish a large teeter-totter.
- There are a number of uses for this tipsy event.

  1. Place the entire group (up to 20 people) in the center of the platform and achieve a balanced position. Ask the group to then move out in each direction so that all the participants end up on the last two boards at each end, in balance. Each touch of the platform during the attempt is counted as a penalty. During a second attempt see if the group can accomplish the task incurring less penalties.
  2. Place the entire group around the verge of the platform, in balance. Ask them to move 360° from their personal position around the platform without letting the platform ends touch. This is a very difficult task. Perhaps a 180° movement would be more realistic.

Specifications:
- The side boards measure 6" x 6" x 14'. The fulcrum board measures 6" x 6" x 6'. The crossing boards measure 2" x 8" x 6'. Some bracing beneath the platform in the form of 2 x 4 truss construction is also necessary.
- Use deck screws to attach the top boards, which should be pressure-treated lumber.

Rules and Safety Concerns:
- Do not allow any fooling around on the platform that would cause someone to be thrown to the ground. There is a large temptation to use this event as a launching platform.
- No one stands near the ends of the platform during use because of the possibility of crushing a foot.

Individual and Group Issues:
- Emotional and physical balance
- Individual influences on the group outcome
- Clear communication
- Weight

Notes

Example Processing Questions:
- How did individuals movement affect the whole group?
- How were you able to stay focused throughout this element?
- What resources did you have? How did you utilize your resources?

Sequencing of Event:
- This element may come at the early stages of initiatives. Don't start with this initiative as it can be very difficult. The group will benefit from the experience of less difficult problem-solving initiatives first.

Appendix I

Index of Ropes Course Program Forms

NOTE: *The following forms are provided as "samples." We cannot verify that they cover legalities for every activity, location, or principality. We highly suggest that adequate counsel be sought to be certain that necessary requirements for your specific situation and location are covered.*

- **Contract Course Notes**

- **Information Letter**

- **Informed Consent for Challenge Ropes Course**

- **Assumption of Risk and Informed Consent**

- **Voluntary Release Form**

- **Participant Information and Release of Liability (Adventureworks, Inc.)**

- **Applicant Information and Release Form (On Course, Inc.)**

- **Medical Information Form**

- **Accident Report**

- **Ropes Course Equipment Check In/Out Sheet**

- **Ropes Course Evaluation**

- **Facilitator Hour Log (Adventureworks, Inc.)**

- **Facilitator Workshops & Training Log (Adventureworks, Inc.)**

Contract Course Notes

Contact:

Initial Contact Date: _____

Contact Person _____

Organization _____

Mailing Address _____

Business Phone: ( ) _____

Home Phone: ( ) _____

Fax: ( ) _____

Client (if applicable): _____

Course Date(s): _____ Confirmed _____

Hours _____

Participants: Minimum _____ Maximum _____

Evaluations Sent _____

Thank You Note _____

Course Description: *HIGH   LOW   BOTH*

_____
_____
_____

Special Needs: _____
_____

Contractee Provides: Food _____Transportation _____

We Provide: Food _____Transportation _____

Logistical Notes: _____
_____

Quoted Price: _____

Nonrefundable deposit: _____ Due: _____ Terms: _____

Memo:

Office Records

Course Number _____

Course Coordinator _____

Contract Sent _____

Contract Received _____

Deposit Received _____

Deposit Receipt Sent _____

Pre-Course Packet Sent
_____ Medical Form
_____ Map
_____ Assumption of Risk
_____ Clothing List
_____ Parental Consent
_____ Informed Consent
_____ Information Letter

Invoice Sent _____

Balance Received _____

Initial Receipt Sent _____

Information Letter

Dear Participant,

Congratulations on your enrollment in the Ropes Course experience! We look forward to getting to know you! In preparing for the course, here are some things to consider:

Attire

There is a good possibility that you could get dirty during the day. Please wear clothing and shoes that you will not mind "scuffing" up a bit. During rainy or wet days we generally continue and use rain ponchos (you supply) when required. We take shelter during severe weather, such as thunderstorms.

Clothing should be:
- Loose
- Comfortable
- Casual
- Durable
- Long pants or sweats are preferred during the cooler seasons
- In very hot weather, shorts with shoes and socks may be preferred
- Layered (layers suitable to the season will allow you to be comfortable all day)

Shoes should be:
- Low heeled
- Comfortable, such as running shoes or sneakers
- Suitable for the weather conditions (consider mud, rain, cold, etc.)

Jewelry, watches and non-prescription sunglasses:
- Are best left at home or in your car in a safe place, as we ask that they be removed before going out to the Ropes Course.

Glasses and contact lens wearers:
- Take any precautions that you would normally take when participating in outdoor activities to protect your eyes and your eye wear.

Tobacco products, gum and candy:
- Are not allowed on the Ropes Course or during activities (for safety reasons)
- Tobacco may be allowed in a separate area during breaks only

Who May Participate?

Anyone of "normal" physical condition, age 8* and up may participate. If you have any physical conditions out of the ordinary, please inform us and note it on the Medical Information Form, so that we may assist you in performing activities safely. Our rule on the course is "Honor your Body." The activities are designed to be played by those of varying levels of physical fitness, and our qualified staff will assist you in taking the next step in learning and growth.

---

*Permission from course director may occasionally be obtained for younger children.

Informed Consent for Challenge Ropes Course

Risks	Prevention	Solution/Treatment
1. Getting hit by a falling object.	Be alert. Look up before walking near or under course. Wear a helmet.	Inform Staff of injuries for assistance.
2. Hair, clothing, or jewelry getting caught in pulleys or other parts of the challenge course.	Have long hair tied back. Remove rings, dangling earrings, watches, etc., and wear proper clothing, (i.e., avoid loose sleeves.)	If caught, remain calm and ask Staff for assistance.
3. Injuries or discomfort caused by improper wearing of harness.	Tie harness as secure as possible and check for any loosening throughout the day. Have tied harness checked by two different Staff members.	If you have any questions or doubts, ask Staff for assistance.
4. Scrapes and cuts.	Climb within abilities. Wear proper clothing.	Inform Staff of any injuries.
5. Death or serious injury.	Wear proper safety gear. Check to see if carabiners are secure. Make sure belayer is ready BEFORE you climb.	Inform Staff of any injuries.

I have read and understand the risks listed above and how to avoid them and agree to take an active part to protect myself and my fellow participants during this activity. I realize there are other risks and/or dangers that may exist and I will avoid these also, and I will not participate in unsafe practices and I will inform the Staff of any dangers known to me that may cause injury to myself or others.

Furthermore, I agree to respect the rights and feelings of the other participants and staff and to act in a supportive and caring manner during my participation of this event.

I understand that I should do nothing that may harm the environment or destroy its natural beauty, so that anyone that follows me may enjoy what nature can provide.

I understand that I have the right to not participate if I don't feel physically or emotionally safe.

I have read all of this Informed Consent and understand that I may be dismissed from participation for refusing to follow any of the above.

Signed_____ Date _____

_____ Date _____
Signature of parent/guardian (if under 18)

Please Print:

Name _____ Phone (_____)_____

Address _____

_____ Age _____

Assumption of Risk and Informed Consent

I, _____ , fully understand

that my participation in _____

sponsored by _____ could result

in accidental injury or death. Also, my participation requires that I be of good

physical condition and I do hereby accept all responsibility for my own

physical well-being. Being fully aware of the degree of risk and injury to

myself, I hereby release _____

and all of its employees and instructors of any liability resulting from

accident or injury incurred by myself while participating in these activities.

Print name _____

Signature _____

Date _____

Instructor or witness _____

Date _____

Participants under 18:

Signature of parent or guardian _____

Date _____

Print name of parent or guardian _____

Voluntary Release Form

By signing this release form I agree to release and hold harmless *your company name* , its agents, assistants, employees, and co-sponsors including but not limited to: *company you are doing the training for or in conjunction with* and its employees or agents, for any damage or injuries, physical or mental, which I might incur as a result of my voluntary decision to participate in the "Ropes Course Experience" held at: *name of facility, location of facility, city, state* on *date* .

If I do voluntarily choose to participate in the Ropes Course, I recognize that there is a significant element of risk in any adventure, sport, or activity associated with the outdoors. Knowing the inherent risks, dangers, and rigors involved in the activities, I certify that I am fully capable of participating in the activities.

I assume full responsibility for myself for bodily injury, death, loss of personal property, and expenses thereof, as a result of my negligence, or other risks, including but not limited to those caused by the obstacle course, the terrain, the weather, my athletic and physical condition, and other participants.

By signing this release form, I agree that if I do sustain any physical injury or mental damage of any nature as a result of my voluntary decision to participate in the Ropes Course, I voluntarily agree to hold harmless and release the above named parties from any liability therefore and that this release is binding on my heirs and assigns.

I acknowledge that I have been given the opportunity to ask questions regarding any aspect of this release form and by signing in the space provided below I do acknowledge that I have read completely and fully understand all aspects of this release form and agree to its terms in its entirety.

_____

Print name

_____   _____

Signature   Date

_____   _____

Signature of parent or guardian (if under 18)   Date

_____

Print name of parent or guardian

_____

Address of participant

_____

Telephone

ADVENTUREWORKS, INC.

A CENTER FOR EXPERIENCE-BASED LEARNING

1300 Narrows of The Harpeth Rd., Kingston Springs TN, 37082

615-952-4720

PARTICIPANT INFORMATION & RELEASE OF LIABILITY

DISCLOSURE

ADVENTUREWORKS programs involve a variety of activities that often include warm-ups, games, group initiative problems, high and low ropes course elements, and other rigorous physical adventure activities. The level of participation in an ADVENTUREWORKS activity is at all times completely voluntary and up to the individual's choice. Yet there is a risk, which must be assumed by each participant, that he or she may suffer an emotional or physical injury or disability.

Policy for participation in all ADVENTUREWORKS programs requires that every participant have health/accident insurance coverage. In addition, certain health/medical information must be made known to the instructor(s) conducting programs, so that they are prepared to respond appropriately if the need arises.

This information will be read by your Adventureworks facilitators ONLY and kept in strict confidence. (If participating as an employee from an organization you may ensure confidentiality by returning this form prior to program in a sealed envelope with your name on the outside.)

PART I. GENERAL INFORMATION (please print)

1. Name _____

2. Street _____ City _____ State _____ Zip _____

3. Home Phone _____ Work Phone _____

4. Age _____   5. Height _____   6. Weight _____

7. Male ☐   Female ☐

8. Person to be notified in case of emergency _____
   Name

Full address _____

Area Code _____ Home Telephone _____

Business Telephone (_____)_____ Relationship _____
   Area Code

PART II. MEDICAL COVERAGE & HISTORY

1. Do you have health/accident insurance?   YES ☐   NO ☐

Name of company? _____

2. Please check if you have or have had any problems with the following:

1 ☐ Problem with hearing - require hearing aid

2 ☐ Dizzy spells, fainting, convulsions

3 ☐ Shortness of breath, asthma on exertion

4 ☐ Chest pains on exertion

5 ☐ Palpitation of the heart, irregular heart beat, heart murmurs

6 ☐ Low or High blood pressure

7 ☐ Heart attack

8 ☐ Hernia

9 ☐ Chronic pain in neck, back, shoulders, arms or legs

10 ☐ Broken bones, joint dislocations, serious sprains, weakness of muscles

11 ☐ Joint pains, swelling or stiffness without injury

12 ☐ Any sever injury to head, chest, internal organs

13 ☐ Any surgeries

14 ☐ Severe illness requiring hospitalization or prolonged incapacitation

15 ☐ Episodes of depression, anxiety, hysteria, nervousness

16 ☐ History of diabetes, thyroid trouble, bleeding problems

17 ☐ Currently on any medications?   If so, what? _____

18 ☐ Special dietary restrictions

19 ☐ Hypoglycemia

If you marked any of the above, please list details below according to item number. Please be specific! (e.g. Include item #, dates, names of medications, history of condition, etc.)

_____

_____

_____

Any other conditions that might effect your safe participation in this program?_____

_____

_____

Are you allergic to any of the following?
    Medication (e.g. penicillin, aspirin, sulfa, etc.)_____
    Insect bites (e.g. bee stings, etc.)_____
    other: (e.g. materials, etc.)_____

If so, what is the nature of the reaction?_____

_____

RELEASE OF LIABILITY

I understand that parts of the ADVENTUREWORKS program may be physically/emotionally demanding. I affirm that my health is good, and that I am not under a physician's care for any undisclosed condition that bears upon my fitness to participate in ADVENTUREWORKS activities. I understand that the level of participation in ADVENTUREWORKS activity is at all times completely voluntary and up to the individual's choice. Also, I recognize the inherent risk of injury or disability in ADVENTUREWORKS activities and understand that each participant must assume the risk of injury that could result from any of the activities. I release ADVENTUREWORKS, INC., and its staff members, principals, and board from all liability for any injury to me from participation in ADVENTUREWORKS activities.

Date_____

_____
Participant's Signature

Above name PRINTED_____

_____
Parent or Guardian's Signature (if participant is under 18 years)

PHOTO/MEDIA RELEASE

I grant to ADVENTUREWORKS the right to use, reproduce, assign, and/or distribute photographs, films, videotapes, and sound recordings of myself, for use in materials they may create. I understand that good faith efforts will be made to contact me and to obtain final approval of any materials proposed for such use.

Date_____

Signature_____

On Course, Inc.

Applicant Information and Release Form

The On Course, Inc. Applicant Information and Release Form <u>MUST</u> be signed with <u>NO</u> additions, deletions or changes, for the participant to take part in the On Course, Inc. Challenge Course activities. We want to make sure you understand the risks in Challenge Course activities and have carefully thought through whether you want to participate.

<u>Please Print</u>

Participant's Name: _____ Age: _____

Address: _____ City: _____ Zip: _____

Home Phone: (_____) _____ Business Phone: (_____) _____

Do you have any health problem or disability that may affect your ability to participate in the ON COURSE, INC. program? If yes, please explain: _____

_____

_____

Please provide the following information in case of an emergency:

Person to notify: _____ Phone: (_____) _____

List allergies, if any: _____

_____

Medication(s) currently taking: _____

_____

Health/Medical Insurance Carrier: _____ Policy #: _____

RELEASE FORM: The ON COURSE, INC. program that you have signed up for involves physically and emotionally demanding activities in an outdoor setting. It includes climbing, jumping and other rigorous activities on natural and man made structures that are on the ground or at low, medium or high distances from the ground. You will be working with ON COURSE, INC. Instructors and with others in your group. It is possible that you may be injured while participating in the program either because of your own conduct, conduct of others in the group, conduct of ON COURSE, INC., or the condition of the premises. We want to make sure that you understand the risks of injury before you decide to participate in the program. It is required that you read the following very carefully, make sure you understand it and sign it before you begin participating in the program.

I AM FULLY AWARE THAT THE <u>*ON COURSE, INC.*</u> PROGRAM THAT I AM CHOOSING TO PARTICIPATE IN INCLUDES RIGOROUS PHYSICAL ACTIVITIES. I AM ALSO AWARE THAT THERE ARE RISKS OF PHYSICAL INJURY OR HARM FROM PARTICIPATING IN THE <u>*ON COURSE, INC.*</u> PROGRAM. I VOLUNTARILY ELECT TO PARTICIPATE IN THE PROGRAM AND TO ASSUME THE RISKS OF INJURY OR HARM THAT COULD RESULT FROM PARTICIPATION. ON MY OWN BEHALF, AND ON BEHALF OF MY PERSONAL REPRESENTATIVES AND HEIRS, I HEREBY RELEASE <u>*ON COURSE, INC.,*</u> ITS OFFICERS, EMPLOYEES, CONSULTANTS, AGENTS, AND DIRECTORS FROM ALL LIABILITY FOR ANY INJURY OR HARM TO ME FROM PARTICIPATING IN THE <u>*ON COURSE, INC.*</u> PROGRAM. WHETHER THE INJURY OR HARM IS CAUSED BY THE NEGLIGENCE OF <u>*ON COURSE, INC.*</u> OR OTHERWISE. I HAVE READ AND UNDERSTAND THIS RELEASE OF LIABILITY. I VOLUNTARILY SIGN IT. I HEREBY GIVE PERMISSION FOR <u>*ON COURSE, INC.*</u> TO ADMINISTER BASIC FIRST AID OR TO SEEK APPROPRIATE MEDICAL ASSISTANCE FOR THE PARTICIPANT LISTED ABOVE.

_____   _____

PARTICIPANT SIGNATURE (all participants must sign)   Date

_____   _____

PARENT/GUARDIAN SIGNATURE IF PARTICIPANT IS YOUNGER THAN 18   Date

ON COURSE, INC.
23382 LA COSTA COURT, AUBURN, CALIFORNIA 95602 FON & FAX (916) 268-1259
Installation, Servicing, Training, Inspecting, and Facilitating Challenge Courses.

This is not legal advice, only an example.
Seek advice from counsel before using any documents presented here.

Medical Information Form

I. General Information (Please Print)

Name _____ Today's Date _____

Address _____
street number   city   state   zip

Home phone _____ Work phone _____

Male ( ) Female ( ) Height _____ Weight _____ Date of Birth _____

Sponsoring Organization _____ Smoker? Yes or No

II. Medical Information

1. Family Physician _____ Phone _____

   Address _____

2. Person to be notified in case of emergency _____

   Address _____

   H. phone _____ W. phone _____ Relationship _____

3. Date of last Tentanus Booster _____

   List any medicines to which you are allergic _____

   _____

   List any other allergies (food, insect bites, poison ivy, etc.)_____

   _____

   Are you allergic to bee stings? If yes, do you carry medicine? _____

   Name of medicine _____ Nature of reactions _____

III. Medical History

1. Name any illness or condition for which you are now undergoing treatment and list any
   medications that you are currently taking _____

   _____

2. If you have had any of the following conditions, state the year of occurrence and the body location in which it occurred

Hernia _____   Fracture _____

Dislocation _____   Sprain or Strain _____

3. Name any injury, illness, or disability not mentioned, and year of occurrence

_____

4. If you have ever been hospitalized, list information below

Date   *Name & location of hospital*   *Illness or injury*

_____

_____

5. If you have, or have had any of the following symptoms or conditions, circle "Yes," *underline specifics,* and provide sufficient details. If not, circle "No."

a) YES   NO   Dizziness, Loss of consciousness, or Recurrent headaches

b) YES   NO   Eye, Ear, Nose, Throat, Tonsils, or Sinus Symptoms

c) YES   NO   Impairment of Sight, Hearing, or Speech

d) YES   NO   Chronic cough, Bronchitis or Asthma, Coughing up Blood, Close contact with tuberculosis

e) YES   NO   Chest pain, Shortness of breath, Palpitation, Swelling of ankles, Heart murmur, Heart disease, High or Low blood pressure

f) YES   NO   Reaction to bee stings

g) YES   NO   Sensitivities/allergies to: Horse serum (tetanus antitoxin), Sulfa, Penicillin, or any other drug

h) YES   NO   Symptoms relating to the Gastrointestinal Tract (diarrhea, recurring abdominal pain, passing of blood, ulcer of stomach or duodenum)

i) YES   NO   Severe menstrual cramps or associated problems, current pregnancy

j) YES   NO   Albumin, Sugar or blood in urine, Kidney stone, Frequency in urinating, Bed wetting, or other Urinary difficulties

k) YES   NO   Muscle, Joint, Knee, Back pain, Bursitis, Arthritis, Sciatica

l) YES   NO   Benign or Malignant growth or tumor

m) YES   NO   History of Diabetes, Thyroid imbalance, Hypoglycemia

n) YES   NO   Episodes of Depression, Anxiety, Hysteria, Nervousness

o) YES   NO   Special dietary restrictions (i.e. diabetic, vegetarian)

Provide details in regard to any questions to which you have circled "Yes"

_____

_____

_____

_____

IV. Insurance

We do not provide sickness or accident insurance for participants. Therefore, it is each participant's responsibility to be covered by his/her own hospitalization policy.

1. Are you covered by any hospitalization or medical care policy? _____

2. Indicate the name of insurance company issuing policy _____

    Policy or certificate number _____

V. Signature (if participant is under 18 years of age, parent or guardian must sign)

I am aware of my past and present health and fitness in relationship to strenuous activity. I fully understand the rigorous nature of the Ropes Course Experience. In the event of an accident or emergency that renders me unable to communicate, I grant my permission for any medical care, operations and/or anesthesia might might become necessary.

Failure to complete all portions of this form could result in injury or compound the damage of an existing injury.

_____   _____

Date   Signature

Accident Report

Instructor/Supervisor _____ Course Director _____

Victim- M / F (Name) _____ Age _____

Date _____ Activity _____ Time _____

Geographic Location (on course) _____

Part I.

A. _____ Injury _____ Illness _____ Incident (describe) _____

(Choose details from Part II & III.)

B. Medical Evacuation? ____ *NO* __*YES* Method _____

Medical Facility? ____*NO*__*YES* Doctor's Name _____

Day(s) Lost? ____*NO*__*YES* How many? ___Course Completed _____

Pre-existing cond.? ____*NO*__*YES* Course #___ Length _____ Day _____

C. Weather: Temp ____Clouds___Precip ___ Winds ____Visibility _____

NARRATIVE: (Describe how the accident happened, include medical treatment provided, and disposition of victim. Attach physician's report if victim was examined and/or treated by one.)

_____

_____

_____

_____

_____

_____

ANALYSIS: (Include any recommendations, suggestions and observations)

_____

_____

_____

_____

_____

Part II.

A. TYPE OF INJURY OR ILLNESS *(may be duplicated from Part I)*

_____ Abrasion	_____ Frostbite	_____ AMS (Altitude)
_____ Burn	_____ Laceration	_____ Allergy
_____ Concussion	_____ Puncture	_____ Dermatitis
_____ Contusion	_____ Sprain	_____ Fever
_____ Fatigue	_____ Strain	_____ Gastrointestinal
_____ URI (Resp)	_____ Infection	_____ Hyperthermia
_____ Urinary Tract	_____ Hypothermia	

Other: _____

B. PROGRAM ACTIVITY

_____ Camp	_____ Canoe/Kayak	_____ Climb/Rappel
_____ Cooking	_____ Cycle	_____ Hike
_____ Raft	_____ Ropes	_____ Ski
_____ Swim	_____ Van/Vehicle	

Other: _____

Part III.

A. CONTRIBUTING FACTORS or type of Near Miss/Incident
(may check more than one)

_____ Clothing	_____ Fatigue	_____ Slip/Fall
_____ Darkness	_____ Speed	_____ Misbehavior
_____ Drugs	_____ Lightning	_____ Instruction
_____ Equipment	_____ Medication	_____ Supervision
_____ Exceed Abilities	_____ Missing/Lost	_____ Unbelayed
_____ Falling Rock/Object	_____ Protection Failure	_____ Unfit Student
_____ Fast Water	_____ Psychological	_____ Weather
_____ Failed to Follow Instructions		

Other: _____

Ropes Course Equipment

Check In/Out Sheet

Lead Facilitator _____ Today's Date _____

Group/Organization _____ No. of Participants _____

Group Date _____ Date & Time Due Back _____

1. Lead Facilitator _____

2. _____

3. _____

4. _____

Signatures:

4. Returned to _____ on _____
                                Equipment Manager   Date

3. Returned to _____ on _____
                         Eq. Mgr./Prg. Coord./Director   Date

2. Received by _____ on _____
                               Lead Facilitator   Date

1. Received from _____ on _____
                        Eg. Mgr./Prg.Coord./Director   Date

CAREFULLY CHECK ALL EQUIPMENT BEFORE USING IT AND BEFORE STORING IT AFTER USE!

Belay Ropes & Static Lines:

- Check for fraying, breakage, and wear
- Double check any stain or discoloration
- Remove all knots after use
- Do not store wet rope
- **Record actual hours used on this form**

All metal pieces of equipment:

- Check for dents, wear, and possible defects
- Check for possible weak points
- Check for any sign of questionable integrity
- Check for corrosion

Dynamic Belay Ropes

Hours   *Hours*

Green	(155")	_____	_____	Gr/Blue	(185")	_____	_____
Blue	(148")	_____	_____	Yellow	(171")	_____	_____
Yel/Gr	(100")	_____	_____	White	(?)	_____	_____

Static Belay Ropes   *Hours*   *Comments*

Flying Squirrel	_____	_____
A/C—D/C	_____	_____

Static Lines

Crab Claws	_____	out of 8
Running Zip	_____	out of 1
May Pole	_____	out of 1
Nitro Crossing	_____	out of 2
Mohawk Traverse	_____	out of 1
Zip Line Lanyard	_____	out of 1
Zip Haul-Rope	_____	out of 1

Block & Tackle

Spin/Static Pulley	_____	out of 6 (Climbing Wall is equipped)
Zip Line Pulley	_____	out of 1
Gold Rosas	_____	out of 5 (Climbing Wall is equipped)
Rapid Links	_____	out of 3

Carabiners

Steel locking	_____	out of 26
Aluminum locking	_____	out of 9
Auto-lock	_____	out of 2

Belay & Rappel Devices

ATC	_____	out of 1
Tuber	_____	out of 1
Sticht Plate	_____	out of 3
Gri Gri	_____	out of 1
Figure 8	_____	out of 1

Harnesses

Seat Harness	_____	out of 26
Full Body Harness	_____	out of 2

Safety Equipment

Helmets	_____	out of 13
Rescue Bag	_____	out of 1 (80' rope, Rescue 8, Etrier, Safety
First Aid Kit	_____	out of 2 Knife and 2 steel carabiners)

Miscellaneous

Rope Tarp	_____	out of 1
Fidget Ladder	_____	out of 1
Trapeze	_____	out of 1
4-way Tug Rope	_____	out of 1

Ropes Course Evaluation

GROUP: _____ DATE _____

FACILITATORS: _____

We are constantly growing and seeking to improve the quality of our programs. Your feedback, both positive and negative, is important in helping us to achieve this goal. This evaluation is optional - please be open and honest.
Please rate each question from 1-5, with 5 being the highest, and write in additional comments.

1 2 3 4 5   Were you satisfied with the ropes course?

1 2 3 4 5   Would you recommend this course to a friend?

1 2 3 4 5   Was the ropes course worth the time and money?

1 2 3 4 5   Were the facilitators well prepared for this course?

1 2 3 4 5   Did the facilitators make the goals and objectives of the course clear at the beginning?

1 2 3 4 5   Did the facilitators encourage questions?

1 2 3 4 5   Were the facilitators supportive of your group?

1 2 3 4 5   Did the facilitators demonstrate a high degree of safety consciousness?

PLEASE TAKE YOUR TIME IN ANSWERING THESE QUESTIONS:

1. What did you like about the ropes course?

2. What did you learn about yourself as an individual? As a group member?

3. What suggestions or changes would you make?

4. How was this course useful to your group?

ADVENTUREWORKS, INC.
A CENTER FOR EXPERIENCE-BASED LEARNING

Facilitator Hour Log

NAME _____

Name of group	Observed/ Facilitated	Date(s)	Total # of Hours	Co-facilitator

Observation/Facilitation Requirements ONLY

Basic Facilitator Status
Observe/assist for minimum of 40 hours (5 full days) with a lead facilitator.
Co-facilitate a minimum of 4 programs with lead facilitator. (Depending on experience may be reduced to 2 programs.)

To Maintain Basic Facilitator Status
Facilitate a minimum of 2 groups for Adventureworks, Inc. per year.

Lead Facilitator Status
Obtain Basic Facilitator Status.
Minimum of 40 hours (5 full days) working as assistant/co-facilitator with a lead facilitator.

Maintain Lead Facilitator Status
Facilitate a minimum of 5 groups per year for and at Adventureworks, Inc.
Attend both a soft and hard skills weekend training each year.

To Regain Lead Facilitator Status
Work with a lead facilitator for a minimum of 2 program days and receive his or her approval or attend a weekend facilitator training, Adventure Foundations Training or a Groupworks Training.

ADVENTUREWORKS, INC.
A CENTER FOR EXPERIENCE-BASED LEARNING

Facilitator Workshops & Training Log

NAME _____

Name of Workshop/Training	Date(s)/Hours	Description and Sponsor or if not offered by Adventureworks

Workshop Training Requirements ONLY

Basic Facilitator Status
Attend an Adventure Foundations Training.

To Maintain Basic Facilitator Status
Attend minimum of 1 Weekend Facilitator Training per year.

Lead Facilitator Status
Attend an Adventure Foundations Training.
Attend a Groupworks Training.
Attend both a soft and hard skills Weekend Facilitator Training.

Maintain Lead Facilitator Status
Attend a minimum of 1 soft and 1 hard skills Weekend Facilitator Training per year.

To Regain Lead Facilitator Status
Attend a weekend facilitator training, Adventure Foundations Training or a Groupworks Training or work with a lead facilitator for a minimum of 2 program days and receive his or her approval.

Appendix II

Ropes Course
One-Day Schedule

This schedule is designed as a starting point for a day on *your* course. Your imagination, creativity, and goals will determine your final schedule. Make sure you have received and reviewed the proper forms prior to beginning your day. Provide breaks for your group when appropriate.

8:30   Opening—Welcome and Introductions of Staff

Name Games
- Toss-a-Name
- Silly Syllable

Housekeeping
- Bathroom
- Environmental
- Medical
- Remove Jewelry
- Staff Roles
- Tobacco Policy

Standards for the Course
- No alcohol, non-prescription drugs
- Give staff undivided attention
- Commit to do your best
- Keep statements positive, no hurtful words
- Tell Staff if you are hurting—emotionally or physically
- Be respectful of others

Goals
- Have safe fun!!
- Be an active part of the group
- Take care of yourself—physically and emotionally
- Stretch yourself beyond your comfort zone

Create a Team Spirit Word (or sound)

Partner Tag (Fast Walking!)

Notes

Moon Ball

Introduction of the Experiential Learning Cycle

Goal Setting
• individual
• group

Stretches
• stork stretch
• windmill stretch

Spotting—Lifting
• demonstration
• practice

Boiling Peanut Butter

People-to-people

All Aboard

Nitro Crossing

Wild Woozey

Trust Sequence
• Tic-Toc
• Wind-in-the-Willow
• Trust Fall (*only* if the group has demonstrated readiness)

11:30   Lunch

Re-focus Activities
• Johnny, OOPS, Johnny
• Bang-Bang, you're dead

Equipment instruction and demonstration

Ground School

High Course

Pamper Pole

Wall

4:30   Closing
• WEB of Appreciation
• Feedback to others

5:00   Finished

Ropes Course
Two-Day Schedule

This schedule is designed as a starting point for a two day experience on *your* course. Your imagination, creativity, and goals will determine your final schedule. Make sure you have received and reviewed the proper forms prior to beginning your day. Provide breaks for your group when appropriate.

DAY 1:

8:30   Opening
- Welcome
- Introductions of Staff

Name Games
- Echo Name Game
- Ball Toss

Housekeeping

Standards

Goals

Create a Team Spirit Word (or sound)

Octopus Tag

Birthday Line Up!

Moon Ball (or other activity that provides entry to goals)

Goal Setting
- individual
- group

Stretches—Warm Up
- name game w/stretches

Spotting—Lifting
- demonstration
- lifting

Traffic Jam

Trolley's

Group 1	*Group 2*
Nitro Crossing	Wild Woozey
Wild Woozey	Nitro Crossing

Human Machine

11:30   Lunch

Notes

Re-focus Activities
- Copy Cat
- Royal Frog!

Human Machine

Group 1	*Group 2*
Mohawk Walk	Re-Birth
Re-Birth	Mohawk Walk

Trust Sequence
- Tic-Toc
- Wind-in-the-Willows
- Trust Fall (*only* if the group has demonstrated readiness)

Spiders Web

Closing
- individual comments
- evaluations of the day
- any feedback for participants
- hopes for tomorrow

3:30   Finished for the Day

DAY 2:

8:30   Welcome and Check-In
- quick whip-around for feelings

Review from Yesterday
- goals
- standards
- anything not covered previous day

Stretches

People-to-People

Transformer Tag

Object Retrieval

Wall

Equipment instruction and demonstration

11:30 Lunch

Ground School

High Course

Pamper Pole

Solo

Feedback from Day

Human Knot (or other close-out, wrap-up activity)

Closing
- WEB of Appreciation
- Farewells

4:30 Finished

Ropes Course
Pre-Meeting Schedule

This schedule is designed as a starting point for *your* meeting. Your imagination, creativity, and goals will determine your final schedule.

Introductions
- staff
- organization

History of Ropes Course
- overview
- main contributors, i.e. Outward Bound

Purpose of a Ropes Course
- primary goals
- adaptation to individual and group goals

Getting to know your participants
- name game

Provide a sample activity
- Have you ever?

Information about the Ropes Course Day
- general photos
- quotes from former participants
- types of activities
  - low course
  - high course
- typical goals
  - individual challenges
  - relationship building
  - trust building
  - problem-solving
  - team building

Open Discussion/Questions and Answers
Note: Participants may be nervous, so it is very important to generate open discussion and questions to help them feel more comfortable and confident.

Goal Setting—Write on a flip chart or board for everyone to see
- individual goals
- group goals

Paperwork
- clothing list
- informed consent
- medical form
- assumption of risk

Finances
- arrange for or collect payment

Closing
- allow for any left-over questions or concerns
- remind them to bring all forms to the course
- let them know that you are looking forward to seeing them on the ropes course

Notes

Suggested Reading List

Adventure Education *Miles/Priest, Venture Publishing*

All I Really Need to Know I Learned in Kindergarten *Fulghum-Villard Books*

American Red Cross Standard First Aid *The American Red Cross*

Art and Science of Processing Experience, The *Clifford C. Knapp/N. Illinois University*

Back Pocket Adventures, *Rohnke & Grout—Kendall/Hunt Publishing Company*

Bottomless Bag Again, *Rohnke—Kendall/Hunt Publishing Company*

Challenge Course Standards, Second Edition, 1998. Purcellville, VA: A.C.C.T. Standards Committee

Common Practices in Adventure Programming *Compiled and Edited by Williamson/ Johanson, Published by Association of Experiential Education*

Conscious Use of Metaphor in Outward Bound, The *Bacon-Typoe Smith of Colorado*

Cowtails and Cobras II *Rohnke—Kendall/Hunt Publishing Company*

Food for Thought, A Methaphorical Potluck *Georgia College—Kendall/Hunt Publishing Company*

Funn Stuff, Vols. 1–3 *Rohnke—Kendall/Hunt Publishing Company*

Influencing with Integrity *Laborde—Syntony Press*

Joining Together, 5th Edition *Johnson, D. and Johnson, F.—Princeton-Hall, Inc.*

Journal of Experiential Education *Association of Experiential Education*

Learning from Experience through Reflection *Daudelin, Marilyn—Organizational Dynamics*

Magic of Conflict, The *Crum-Simon and Schuster*

Metaphors, The Book *Gass—Kendall/Hunt Publishing Company*

Outdoor Network Newsletter *Moniz/Secunda—Outdoor Network*—No longer available

Outdoor Programming Handbook, The *Watters—Idaho State University Press*

Principle Centered Leadership *Covey—Simon and Schuster*

Quicksilver *Rohnke /Butler—Kendall/Hunt Publishing Company*

Silver Bullets *Rohnke—Kendall/Hunt Publishing Company*

Skilled Facilitator, The *Schwarz—Jossey-Bass Publishers*

Adventure in the Classroom—*M. Henton Project Adventure*

Unlimited Power *Robbins—Simon and Schuster*

Glossary

A.C.C.T.—Association of Challenge Course Technology. A national association of primarily Ropes Course builders, established to set safe building and implementation standards for the field of challenge course construction and operation.

Back-up Cable—A relatively short section of cable that is connected to, or is an integral part of, the belay cable system, and which protects the belay cable in case of bolt failure.

Belay—In a Ropes Course context, the rope or technique that is used to protect a climber from falling to the ground. A belay can be either dynamic or static.

Brake Hand—The dominant hand used by the belayer to slow or stop the rope from going through the belay device or around the belayer's body.

Bungee Cord—Parallel lengths of rubber-band material held in place by a woven nylon sheath (mantle). Used primarily on a Ropes Course as a braking device for the zip wire element or the low course element Spider's Web.

C.B.C.—Challenge by Choice. The freedom to temporarily back-off from participation. *C.B.C.* is not an invitation to opt out.

Cable Clip—(Also known as a cable clamp)—A drop forged galvanized cable connection device.

Carabiner—A steel or alloy link that has a spring loaded gate. For ropes course use, the carabiner should have a locking gate.

Cheeks—The side plates of a *snatch-block* pulley.

Commitment Agreement—A series of positive actions, beliefs, and behaviors that participants agree to working toward while sharing an adventure.

Crab Claws—(Also Lobster or Bear Claws)—A static, single person belay system made of a piece of multiline. It is connected to a participant's harness with a carabiner or girth hitch. Two adjustable loops extend out from the harness with one carabiner in each loop used for lead climbing Ropes Courses in a give-and-go technique.

Dynamic—A rope or system capable of stretching, giving or elongating when stopping a fall or force applied to the system. In a Ropes Course context, it refers to either a type of Ropes Course, a type of belay, or the rope itself.

Dynamic Belay—A bottom (sling shot) belay where a participant's fall is controlled by a belayer. See *Static Belay* for comparison.

Etrier—A type of highly portable, light-weight ladder made of rope, small diameter cable, or webbing—used in caving, rock climbing, and during Ropes Course rescues.

Facilitator—A person who "makes things easier" by:
- clearly and definitely presenting a challenge or situation.
- setting definite perimeters for safety and operation.
- acting as a "video recorder" to assist later debriefing sessions.

Notes

- maintaining a supportive presence but not helping or interfering with the group's process.
- assisting with verbal and emotional sharing of an experience.

Fish Plate—A 2" x 2" galvanized washer used in Ropes Course construction.

Fist Grip—A highly efficient double bolted clamp device used to secure two sections of cable together. More efficient and more expensive than a cable clip.

Flaking a Rope—Making a single turn in a coil, concurrently checking the rope for wear or damage.

G.A.C. 7 x 19—Galvanized *Aircraft Cable*. A high quality, flexible cable made up of seven twisted main strands. Each one of those seven strands are made up of an additional 19 smaller strands.

Galvanized—A type of protective coating, hot dipped onto metal to prevent rusting.

Girdled—The process of girdling occurs when a cable or rope is wrapped tightly around a tree. As the tree grows, the rope or cable cuts into the bark and eventually kills the tree.

GriGri—A mechanical belay device which conveniently and definitely arrests the belay rope if the belayer loses control.

Ground School—A low practice area which simulates a high static ropes setting. Can also be any place where an assembled group goes to practice belaying and other high course procedures.

Guys—Angled (usually 45 degree) cables that connect from a ground anchor to an erect pole or tree providing support.

Hawser Lay—A laid rope constructed of three or more main twisted strands, constructed in such a way that successively smaller strands are twisted in opposition to each other. More elastic than kernmantle rope, but not as supple or as strong.

Industry Standards—A set of standards for operation and construction agreed upon by experts in the field. Refer to A.C.C.T.

Initiatives—Unique activities that are problem-solving in nature.

Jus-rite belay (descender)—A nine foot pole (usually treated) approximately 8 to 12 inches in diameter, buried four feet in the ground with five feet out of the ground. The above ground section has a series of three holes drilled at opposite angles; the belay rope runs through these holes. The Just-rite belay is usually set approximately 20 feet back from the element. It creates friction on the rope, making it easy to belay a participant jumping from a Pamper Pole or plank.

Keeper—The connector on a stitch plate that keeps the plate from riding up or down the belay rope; also called a *string*. Alternatively, someone you found who's worth dating again.

Kernmantle—A supple, strong, and decay resistant rope constructed of continuous parallel nylon fibers (kern), or twisted strands surrounded by a woven or braided exterior sheath (mantle).

Knot Tensile Strength—The actual force necessary to break a rope with a knot tied in it. Differs from *tensile strength*.

Lazy Line—Number 4 nylon cord used for hauling a belay rope up and through a shear reduction device.

Lobster Claw—see Crab Claw.

Multiline—A durable hawser-lay rope made of polyester with a polypropylene tracer.

NEB—A *Nut Eye Bolt*. A drop forged bolt used in ropes course construction (usually 5/8 inch in diameter). Varies in length from 4 to 24 inches.

Nylon—A synthetic petroleum product from which high quality ropes are manufactured. Benefits: practically decay free, high tensile strength, considerable elasticity. Drawbacks: susceptible to ultra-violet deterioration.

Pole Class—A number system for grading the diameter of utility poles. Class 1 is larger than class 2, etc.

Polyester (Dacron)—A synthetic material from which rope can be made. Much less stretch than nylon with essentially the same tensile strength.

Polypropylene—A synthetic material from which rope is made. A strong rope but susceptible to UV deterioration. Used to make cargo nets, bridges, trolling lines and webs. Often referred to as "water ski rope;" it floats.

Pressure Treated (PT)—Wood that is pressure injected with a preservative. Also called *Wolmanized.*

Processing, Debriefing, Reviewing—Assisting participants to comprehend and internalize experiences and the lessons learned through those experiences.

Rapid Link—A connecting device that looks like a chain link with a screw gate added. Characterized by great strength and comparatively low price. Used in place of a carabiner when the connector is going to be left on the course.

Rappel—A controlled slide down a single or double rope using a mechanical friction device.

Reeve—To thread a string or rope or cable through something, as in "reeving the cable through an eye bolt."

Retired Rope—Climbing rope that is no longer serviceable as a belay rope. Can be used for games or initiative problems, but should be marked noticeably so that it is not mistaken for a belay rope in service.

ROSA—A Ropes Course pulley developed by Project Adventure. Acronym for *Really Outstanding Safety Attachment.*

Safe Working Load (SWL)—The SWL represents 1/5 or 20 percent of the tensile strength of a rope, bolt, clamp, etc.

Serving Sleeve—A simple piece of galvanized metal that crimps the working end of the cable to the standing end to prevent loose strands from puncturing skin.

Shear—Stretching (and weakening) of the outside fibers of a rope or cable by a weight that produces greater stress on the rope/cable than the actual hanging weight of the initial load.

Sheave—The wheel (steel or aluminum) of a pulley. Pronounced *shiv.*

Shock Loading—A sudden jerk (kinetic load) applied to a rope or cable by a weight that produces greater stress on the rope/cable than the actual hanging weight of the initial load.

Slash Rope—See *Retired rope.*

SLES—A *Shoulder Lay Eye Screw.* A drop forged eye screw that is used for noncritical attachments on a Ropes Course. Pronounced *sleaze.*

SLES Bag—A leather or canvas pouch that attaches to a tree harness. Pronounced *sleaze bag.*

Spaghetti—A term used for stuffing rope into a bag. Done by sticking one end in the bag and stuffing rope continuously in the bag until all rope is stuffed loosely and without coils. This term could also refer to uncoiling a section of rope by grabbing one end and piling it loosely on the ground or tarp.

Spotting—Actively safeguarding the movements of another participant by movement and placement of the spotter's own body.

Staple—A piece of 1/2 inch galvanized metal rod bent into a "U," with points on each end. A staple can be hand sledged into trees or poles to serve as climbing steps. Pre-drilling is sometimes necessary.

Static—No stretch. In a Ropes Course context it refers to either a type of Ropes Course, a type of belay or the rope itself.

Static Belay—A self belay on the Ropes Course whereby the climber attaches him/herself to the belay cable with steel locking carabiners with a short section of rope.

Sticht Plate—A mechanical belay device.

Notes

Strand Vise—Used for connecting cable to an eye bolt. It incorporates a one-way mechanical camming action which allows cable to be inserted but not pulled back out. It is quick and simple to install and affords easy adjustability of the cable.

Swage—A malleable extruded piece of metal used for crimping two lengths of cable together (lap swage), or crimping the cable working end back onto the standing end creating an eye swage.

TEB—*Thimble Eye Bolt*. A drop forged bolt used in Ropes Course construction (usually 5/8 inch with a thimble-shaped head). Varies in length from 4 to 18 inches.

Tensile Strength—The amount of evenly applied force necessary to break a rope in a destructive testing situation. Differs from *Knot tensile strength*. Also applies to webbing cable, carabiners, pulleys, and other mechanical devices.

Three Strand Rope—A rope constructed of three strands twisted together. A three strand rope is less expensive, more abrasion resistant, but less supple than a kernmantle rope.

Tuna Plate—A 4 x 4 inch metal washer used in Ropes Course construction.

UIAA—Acronym for a European organization that maintains quality control testing of alpine gear. Union of International Association of Alpinism.

Useful Life—The length of time a piece of equipment can be safely used. Can also be applied to people, but. . . .

Zax—A slate working tool, also serves as a dynamic scrabble word. This reference has nothing to do with Ropes Courses, but it's something you should know.

Author Biographies

Karl Rohnke

Photo by Nicki Hall.

Karl has an undergraduate degree from Washington and Lee University in Virginia and an honorable doctorate from Unity College in Maine. Karl Rohnke has been an important "player" in the field of experiential/adventure education for over 30 years. He was a watch officer at *Hurricane Island Outward Bound* in 1967 and chief instructor at *NCOBS* until 1971. He left Outward Bound to become one of the founders of the *Project Adventure* (PA) program in Hamilton, MA, and has worked there continuously since that time. During his tenure at PA he served as director and president of the company.

Karl has written over ten books that relate to the field of adventure education, including **Silver Bullets, Cowtails and Cobras, The Bottomless Bag Again!?,** and the **FUNN STUFF** series.

During his time at *Outward Bound* and *Project Adventure,* Karl spent a great deal of occupational effort creating and installing innovative ropes course elements. Many of the ropes course events and safety systems in use today all over the world were created by Karl including: The Pamper Pole, Vertical Playpen, The Mohawk Walk, Studebaker Wrap, Spring Things, and shear reduction belay devices.

Karl currently travels world-wide presenting clinics about the use of games and initiative problems as applied to various pedagogic applications.

Karl, Jim and Catherine have worked together at Georgia College & State University defining and teaching courses toward a master's degree in Outdoor Education.

Catherine Tait

Photo by Jim Wall.

Catherine earned her master's degree in counseling from the University of Oklahoma in 1987. She has over seven years of experience providing direct individual and group counseling services. Her specialty areas are group work, team building, and individual identity development. Catherine has worked in a variety of college counseling centers around the Southeast. She was able to utilize many experiential activities, most noteably the Ropes Course, within the context of counseling. She is an avid traveler and an active participant in outdoor activities such as hiking, backpacking, canoeing and sea kayaking. For the past six years, Catherine has been actively involved in various aspects of ropes course programming. She has developed and conducted numerous Ropes Course facilitator trainings and has worked in conjunction with Jim in the successful management and operation of Wall's Outdoor Associates, Inc. Catherine is currently working at Georgia College & State University as an Academic Adviser and Instructor of Freshmen Studies. She is dedicated to experiential education and consistently incorporates experiential components within the academic arena. She currently holds the rank of captain and has been an active member of the Army National Guard for over nine years and continues to enjoy the opportunity to put leadership and educational concepts to the test. Jim and Catherine were fortunate to meet each other seven years ago and have since forged a partnership for life.

Jim Wall

Photo by Catherine Tait.

Jim earned his master's degree in recreation resources administration from North Carolina State University in 1984. His expertise reflects over twenty-three years of experience, with an emphasis on Ropes Courses and outdoor adventure education. Jim began building Ropes Courses in 1982 and has built numerous courses across the United States in a variety of settings, such as treatment centers, youth development centers, correction facilities, youth camps, and universities. His outdoor recreation experience includes positions as park ranger, naturalist, "at risk" youth counselor, and Parks and Recreation Director. Jim was actively involved in the initial work of the Southeast AEE Task Force in developing peer review standards for outdoor adventure. He has served as faculty member of the North Carolina State University School of Sports Management and has recently served as Chair of the Southeast Association for Experiential Education. Jim currently works at Georgia College & State University as assistant professor in the Health, Physical Education and Recreation Department. He is responsible for creating the only Outdoor Education Administration graduate program in the Southeast. In addition to this creation, Jim has coordinated both the graduate program and the undergraduate program in Outdoor Education as well as having served as the Director of the Outdoor Center. He created Wall's Outdoor Associates, Inc. almost twelve years ago and is actively building Ropes Courses, conducting facilitator training, and designing team building programs.

Index

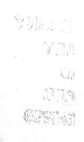